The Politics of Differentiation in Schools

The Politics of Differentiation in Schools is concerned with how schools can provide a more socially just education in the current policy context. Differentiation is positioned as a key point of conflict in the contradictory politics of contemporary schooling. It can act both as a lever to support the most vulnerable/marginalised students and can also work to maintain the privileges of the powerful groups in society. The book explores the 'politics' of various forms of differentiation within and between schools, particularly in relation to social justice. We argue that what is happening in the broader context of society plays a major role in how young people are able to engage with schooling. These issues are brought to life through data collected across three years from principals, teachers, other workers and students at two Australian high schools. These schools attempted to pursue social justice goals through their pedagogical and curricular approaches, their expectations and care towards learners and their extracurricular practices. We contend that spaces for social justice within classrooms, schools and broader education systems will be opened by a politics of differentiation that recognises context and seeks economic, cultural and political justice. Such politics will need to be continually questioned to proliferate new lines of thought and enquiry.

Martin Mills is a Professor in the School of Education at The University of Queensland.

Amanda Keddie is a Professor of Education at Deakin University.

Peter Renshaw is a Professor in the School of Education at The University of Queensland.

Sue Monk is a Lecturer in the School of Education and Professional Studies at Griffith University.

Routledge Research in Education

For a full list of titles in this series, please visit www.routledge.com

173 **Research for Educational Change**
Transforming researchers' insights into improvement in mathematics teaching and learning
Edited by Jill Adler and Anna Sfard

174 **The Development of the Mechanics' Institute Movement in Britain and Beyond**
'A practical education in reach of the humblest means'
Martyn Walker

175 **New Perspectives on Intercultural Language Research and Teaching**
Exploring Learners' Understandings of Texts from Other Cultures
Melina Porto and Michael Byram

176 **Multilingual Digital Storytelling**
Engaging creatively and critically with literacy
Edited by Jim Anderson and Vicky Macleroy

177 **Vocationalism in Further and Higher Education**
Policy, programmes and pedagogy
Edited by Sai Loo and Jill Jameson

178 **Children's Creative Music-Making with Reflexive Interactive Technology**
Adventures in improvising and composing
Edited by Victoria Rowe, Angeliki Triantafyllaki and Francois Pachet

179 **Community-based Media Pedagogies**
Relational Practices of Listening in the Commons
Bronwen Low, Chloe Brushwood Rose, and Paula Salvio

180 **Reclaiming Discipline for Education**
Knowledge, relationships and the birth of community
James MacAllister

181 **The Politics of Differentiation in Schools**
Martin Mills, Amanda Keddie, Peter Renshaw and Sue Monk

The Politics of Differentiation in Schools

Martin Mills, Amanda Keddie,
Peter Renshaw and Sue Monk

Routledge
Taylor & Francis Group
LONDON AND NEW YORK

First published 2017
by Routledge
2 Park Square, Milton Park, Abingdon, Oxon OX14 4RN

and by Routledge
711 Third Avenue, New York, NY 10017

First issued in paperback 2018

Routledge is an imprint of the Taylor & Francis Group, an informa business

British Library Cataloguing in Publication Data
A catalogue record for this book is available from the British Library

Library of Congress Cataloging-in-Publication Data
A catalog record for this book has been requested

ISBN 13: 978-1-138-60462-9 (pbk)
ISBN 13: 978-1-138-79724-6 (hbk)

Typeset in Galliard
by Apex CoVantage, LLC

For John: An inspirational educator

Contents

Acknowledgements

We would like to acknowledge the teachers and students at Red Point State High School and Crimson State High School and thank them for their support, dedication and willingness to participate in the research. We also recognise the contributions of our colleagues David Geelan, Pam Christie and Christina Gowlett, who worked on the design of the project and data collection. We are appreciative of the editorial support provided by Ruth Leach in the preparation of the final manuscript. We thank Springer for the permission to republish sections of 'Beyond Culturalism: Addressing Issues of Indigenous Disadvantage through Schooling' from *Australian Educational Researcher*. We would also like to thank the Australian Research Council for the Discovery Grant (DP1093082) which made this research possible. We also thank Christina Low for her patience in waiting for the delivery of this manuscript.

1 The politics of differentiation

On our first visit to Red Point State High School, one of the schools included in our research, we parked near a grassy verge upon which stood two flagpoles. On one an Australian flag blew gently in a tropical breeze. The other was bare. At the time we were not aware of the controversial significance of these two poles. Two years later when we had completed our research, three flagpoles stood in this same location. In many ways the story of the flagpoles represents a number of the concerns we raise throughout the book in relation to the politics of differentiation, inclusion and social justice. We learnt on this first visit that the Indigenous liaison worker at the school had been lobbying for three flagpoles because of the need to recognise both Aboriginal *and* Torres Strait Islander peoples at the school. Each of these Australian Indigenous groups is represented by a different flag. Her argument was that the school was always going to fly the Australian flag, and that it could not, without being exclusionary, fly just one Indigenous flag on the remaining pole. She argued that both flags should be flown.

This had been a bitter issue amongst the staff, with some resisting such a change because they wished the school to maintain its reputation for having high academic standards, a reputation that could be damaged by being seen as too 'Indigenous friendly'. However, the new principal had expressed a desire for the school to do more for its Indigenous members. This had led, for example, to him making an Acknowledgement of Country[1] at school assemblies, to the dismay of a number on staff. This also led to resentment from some of our student interviewees, who questioned why students from other nationalities could not also have their flags flown at the front of the school. The book is not solely concerned with issues of race, although these are certainly important within its context. However, the flagpole controversy is indicative of the way in which schools wish to be represented to both those working and studying within them and to the external world, and that social justice issues are inevitably tied into such representations. It also foregrounds the tensions that can arise when difference is recognised, where competing claims exist, where messiness is created through different interpretations of who and what should be recognised and how best to remedy matters of misrecognition or marginality. The book engages with these issues as it considers the role of 'differentiation' within contemporary schooling.

The Politics of Differentiation in Schools is concerned with the means by which schools can provide a more socially just education than is currently the case. We take up the issue of 'differentiation' as a key point of conflict in the contradictory politics of contemporary schooling. We argue that calls for differentiation can act both as a lever for progressing the case that schools can do more for their most vulnerable/marginalised students, and that it can also be deployed as a device to reinforce the politics of reproduction and the stratification of schooling to maintain the privileges of the powerful groups in society. One of the concerns related to schooling and differentiation is the way in which contemporary neo-liberal politics treat human activities and problems, such as teaching and learning, the engagement and disengagement with schooling, and the social injustices of racism, misogyny, homophobia and poverty, as problems able to be solved with technical solutions (Bauman 2004). In Queensland, for instance, where our study was located, the State Department of Education created a Teaching and Learning Audit to examine practices in government school classrooms as one such technical solution to the problem of 'low achievement'. Within the Audit, 'differentiation' was seen as being critical to good classroom practice. In this book we adopt a broader view of differentiation by exploring the 'politics' of various forms of differentiation within and between schools, particularly in relation to social justice in schooling.

In taking up the topic of 'differentiation' we address the tension between 'teaching quality' and 'contexts of teaching'. Political and policy leaders have been deploying the mantra that teachers and teaching matter (Barber & Mourshed 2007; Masters 2009), but such advocacy can be used to suggest that context does not matter and that differential funding of schools based on a needs analysis is not required. In focussing on the *politics* of differentiation we want to suggest that differentiation cannot be leached of the political; and that it cannot be considered as a simple technical solution to the problem of low achievement and student disengagement. It cannot be isolated from debates about the distribution of resources, cultural justice and voice. We argue that what is happening in the broader context of society plays a major role in how young people are able to engage with schooling. This broader context relates to matters of injustice, such as poverty and racism, and to matters of education policy.

In the book we recognise that the notion of differentiation can take many forms and relates to many aspects of schooling. We have in recent times been in schools located in both the UK and Australia where there has been an emphasis on differentiation as a means of ensuring all students receive a quality education via excellent classroom practice. However, when we have pushed teachers to discuss differentiation, few are able to clearly define what this means for their practice, and when they do proffer definitions, there is often little consensus amongst these. Two common responses, however, relate to the streaming of classes and differentiated curriculum pathways. Both of these responses have been used to justify providing marginalised students opportunities to succeed. However, at the same time both have been critiqued for entrenching existing inequalities. We have also been witnessing a differentiation of schooling systems where reductive measures of 'performance' have been used to rank systems of schooling across the globe. Some have suggested that such rankings have highlighted injustices by, for example, noting that some systems are high performing but have low levels of equity in terms of the performance of marginalised groups. Others have claimed that these rankings work to instil practices that are designed to lift performance without paying attention to the broader sets of inequities that led to the differential performance in the first place. There has also been differentiation within the system as a result of the market entering into the politics of schooling in relation to, for example, Academies and Free Schools in England, Independent Public Schools in Australia and Charter Schools in the United States. Again, this form of differentiation has been critiqued for the ways in which such forms of autonomy can enable schools to exclude those marginalised learners who 'damage' their results and reputations. At the same time, there are aspects of school autonomy that can foster greater commitment to equity through allowing the creation of innovative and inclusive practices and programs that support marginalised students.

Differentiation is thus a contested term in relation to its contribution to more socially just practices in education. In some cases it is argued that it contributes to social justice by valorising difference; in others it is accused of hindering social justice by entrenching inequalities. In this book we want to explore different notions of differentiation, identify the arguments for and against these understandings and interrogate the differentiated practices in two Australian high schools to consider who wins and who loses from dominant understandings of differentiation. We would suggest that the lessons here have purchase in locations beyond Australia.

Our interest in differentiation arose from two sources. First, we were involved in an Australian Research Council funded research project, *Engaging students: Issues of difference, distribution and recognition in schools*, concerned with the ways in which schools approached issues of social justice. While in the process of selecting schools for the fieldwork, two schools, with which we had formed prior relationships through our teacher education program, encouraged us to work with them to improve their means of engaging all students in productive learning. Secondly, as we were setting up the project, the Teaching and Learning Audit of schools was implemented for the first time across the State with differentiation being identified as a key concern. This focus on differentiation is far from unique to Australia (see Everest 2003). As a consequence we became concerned with the social justice opportunities both opened up and closed down by this policy priority on differentiation.

There are several issues we raise in this introduction by way of laying the groundwork for various discussions of differentiation throughout the book. We note the different forms that differentiation can take with regard to schooling; we indicate that in our concern with social justice we have been drawn to the work of Nancy Fraser (1997; 2009), and those who have worked with and built upon her work (see Lynch 2012); and we also outline some of the key contextual factors that shape the moment in which our study was located. This introduction will also provide an overview of the study and the schools from which the data for this book were sourced.

Pursuing social justice in education: Economic, cultural and political considerations

Fraser (2009) identifies three forms of injustice (economic, cultural and political) that concerned us in undertaking this research. In the first instance, economic injustice is represented by maldistribution, exemplified by people's futures and life opportunities being restricted (or advantaged) by their levels of income, by people having their labour exploited for the benefit of others and by people experiencing high levels of economic deprivation and marginalisation. Addressing this form of injustice, Fraser suggests, will require some form of redistribution of economic resources, including a restructuring of the economic division of labour. Cultural injustice, she argues, is indicated by acts of misrecognition which occur when people experience cultural domination, that is, when they are forced to subjugate their own cultural ways of being and communicating to the (often hostile) norms of the dominant culture, are made invisible or are disrespected as a consequence of being from a particular cultural group. Political injustice occurs when the structures and practices of society, and its institutions, do not accord all of its members a voice. Impacting upon all three dimensions are broader relations and institutions that adjudicate economic, cultural and political justice claims.

These three sets of injustices, related to poverty, various forms of cultural discrimination and lack of political voice, Fraser suggests, all work towards undermining what she calls 'parity of participation' (2009, p.16), a state of affairs where all are able to participate in social life as peers. A socially just education system would therefore work to remove barriers to such participation, both within the practices of schooling and beyond. We note here some of the policy attempts to remove such barriers.

There have been attempts in many countries to address issues of economic injustice in education. In Australia, for example, there has been a major debate about school funding after a review of school funding mechanisms suggested that a differentiated funding system would provide more equitable outcomes from schooling. The assumption underpinning this mooted reform was that an equitable schooling system would be one where schools enrolling students principally from marginalised backgrounds would receive extra financial support compared to those serving more privileged students (Gonski et al. 2011; see Kenway 2013 for discussion). The redistributive justice principles in the Gonski reforms are reflected in previous equity policies in Australia that have sought to improve the school participation and achievement of disadvantaged students through the allocation of extra funding and resources, such as the *Disadvantaged Schools Program*, instituted by the federal government nearly 45 years ago, and the *National Partnership Scheme*, which allocated funding to schools on the basis of their location within low socio-economic communities (see Keddie 2012a). In England, redistributive measures include the 'pupil premium', an extra amount of funding allocated to government schools for every student who is eligible for 'free school meals' or is in or has been in care, and is designed 'to raise the attainment of disadvantaged pupils and close the gap between them and their peers'.[2] However, such redistributive school-focused measures are necessarily limited unless the broader problems facing marginalised young people are also addressed, for example, homelessness, poverty and unstable home-lives. Other redistributive measures have thus taken a more integrated approach to supporting economically disadvantaged students. In many school sites such support might include, for example, specialised counselling and therapy services, family services, parenting education, transportation assistance, housing assistance, childcare services, financial assistance, literacy support and translation services, and other community/social outreach services (Amin et al. 2006; Carswell et al. 2009; Keddie 2012a; Mills & McGregor 2014).

Redistributive justice principles recognise the links between poverty, poor schooling performance, early school leaving and future economic deprivation and social discontent/dysfunction (see Keddie 2012a). Education determines employment credentialing and students' future access to the labour market and the material benefits of the social world (Connell 1994; Mills & Gale 2010). A socially just education in terms of redistribution will, then, assist disadvantaged and marginalised students to achieve on the 'same measuring sticks' of educational achievement (e.g. standardised tests) as their more privileged counterparts so that they can 'mix it with anybody' and eventually access society in the same way that any other student would (Sarra 2003; see also Ladson-Billings 1995). In schools and classrooms, this means not only providing intensive material and human resource support such as that highlighted in the previous paragraphs, but also providing intensive learning support within a context of high expectations to ensure that students from disadvantaged backgrounds achieve on the measures that 'count' (e.g. standardised academic tests). Significant for schools and teachers here is challenging and moving beyond the deficit understandings of these students who typically experience 'watered down' and non-challenging curriculum that can reinscribe their disadvantage (Keddie 2012a; Ladson-Billings 1995; Sarra 2003).

Remedying cultural injustices has often been the target of programs and policies designed to support, for example, students from diverse cultural backgrounds, students with diverse physical abilities, girls and lesbian, gay, bisexual, transgender and intersex (LGBTI) students and to challenge various forms of discrimination such as racism, misogyny and homophobia. The significance of culturally inclusive learning environments that connect with the funds of knowledge specific to marginalised groups is recognised in equity policy and practice as central to this challenge (Zipin, Sellar & Hattam 2012). In Australia, for example, cultural inclusion is prioritised in the *National Goals for Schooling Framework*. The Framework's particular focus is Indigenous marginality and the role of education in valuing the histories and cultures of this group (MCEETYA 2008). Following this, Australia's current National Curriculum has Aboriginal and Torres Strait Islander histories and cultures as one of the three cross-curricula priorities to support the integration of culturally inclusive content across relevant learning areas. At a state policy level in Queensland, cultural inclusivity is promoted through the EATSIPS (Embedding Aboriginal and Torres Strait Islander Perspectives) (Department of Education and Training 2011) framework, where the emphasis is on learning through, as well as about, Indigenous culture. Cultural injustices also occur on multiple planes, for example, Indigenous women and Indigenous LGBTI young people suffer injustices on multiple, often compounding, dimensions and thus require remedial responses on each of these dimensions.

Cultural injustices are also entwined with other forms of injustice. As indicated in the first few paragraphs of the introduction, the representation of Indigenous peoples is important, as is the integration of Aboriginal and Torres Strait Islander histories and cultures into all school curricula. However, economic injustices also impact on Indigenous groups in disproportionate ways. In order to address this, some material support has been provided in Australia to individual Indigenous students and their families in the form of financial support known as Abstudy[3] to counter some of the economic injustices faced by this 'cultural group'. However, there are many cultural injustices that Indigenous young people still face in and beyond school that have major impacts upon their schooling experiences. The same can be said for students from all culturally marginalised backgrounds, for example LGBTI and refugee students. Various chapters in this book consider how the case study schools differentiate their practice, within and outside of the classroom, in order to address forms of cultural injustice.

Political injustices occur when marginalised groups are not accorded a voice and hence are subjected to what Fraser calls misrepresentation. In most western schooling contexts, especially Australia, the UK and the United States, White, western and middle class ways of knowing and being are privileged, and the teaching population is overwhelmingly White and middle-class. There has been a long-held concern about how such contexts can undermine the autonomy of students whose racialised identities are other than the mainstream. In Australia, for example, the under-representation of Indigenous teachers (at less than one per cent of all teachers) is seen to be a contributing factor to the poor academic performance of Indigenous students and their low levels of school retention (relative to their non-Indigenous counterparts) (Keddie 2012b). The Commonwealth government has sought to address this imbalance by increasing the number of Indigenous teachers in Australian schools. The aims of this initiative are to foster greater cultural awareness and understanding of Indigenous issues and to provide Indigenous students with positive role models (DEEWR 2011).

In terms of political injustice in schools, both teachers and students argue that they have little voice in matters that concern them. Considering students first, a significant body of literature addresses the lack of voice that students experience in school (see Baroutsis et al. 2015, 2016; Bragg 2007; Fielding 2004a, 2004b; Mitra 2009; Rudduck & Fielding 2006). Some schools do attempt to incorporate student voice into everyday matters through organisations such as student councils. However, in many cases these attempts are tokenistic (Black 2011) and fail to address what students often perceive as arbitrary disciplinary processes. For example, many young people articulate a sense of being treated 'unfairly' in school and indicate that their inability to appeal decisions made against them played a major role in them 'dropping out' of school (Mills & McGregor 2014). That students who fall into this group are primarily, but not solely, from economically and culturally marginalised groups points to the failure of schools, and the education system, to address injustices on multiple levels.

Attempts to accord students a voice in schools can thus be misappropriated in ways that circumscribe or undermine agency–especially when they are not well integrated or taken seriously within the broader context of the school or when they are driven by adult purposes to, for example, fit with the pragmatic goals of school effectiveness and improvement (Bragg 2007; Fielding 2004a; 2004b). Such misappropriation invariably fails to consider three key issues: 1) authenticity (i.e. taking students' views seriously); 2) inclusion (i.e. including marginalised [or less 'palatable'] student voices); and 3) power (i.e. fostering a sense of teacher-student collaboration and mutual respect) (see Keddie 2014a).

Many teachers also feel that they are rendered voiceless in schools, especially in light of their de-professionalisation, or more accurately, re-professionalisation, around what currently counts as teacher quality and school improvement–scores on standardised tests such as NAPLAN and PISA. Reflecting a very different set of ethics to previous modes of professional judgment and co-operation (see Ball 2003; Gable & Lingard 2015; Lingard & Sellar 2013), these modes of regulation and the ethics of competition and performance they engender undermine teacher autonomy and professionalism. The mistrust and surveillance endemic in the current environment silences teachers' voices and reduces them to their capacity to raise student performance on narrow targets (Ball 2003). While the focus of this book is on the impact of schooling and differentiation on students, it is important that we note that many of the teachers in our two schools claimed a sense of powerlessness when it came to exercising professional judgment.

We draw on Fraser's framework in this book as a productive lens for organising and thinking about the different forms of differentiation within and between schools that might hinder the participation, engagement and outcomes of marginalised students. Given the inter-relatedness of justice issues, we are mindful of the complexities associated with pursuing justice on each dimension–for example, many students suffer injustices on a number of dimensions and thus require multiple remedies to overcome these injustices. We are also especially mindful of the problematics of identity politics on each dimension as potentially reinscribing injustice through reifying difference along reductionist and fixed lines. We thus adopt a critical approach throughout the book to analysing the ways in which the politics of differentiation can work for and against justice imperatives. For example, recognising cultural difference can mean ignoring the complexity of cultural diversity within a specific marginalised category, and assumptions about the political representation of marginalised groups can delimit who can speak on behalf of those groups (Fraser 1997; Keddie 2012a). Taking the flagpole incident with which we began this book, a critical theory of recognition would support the claim that the school needed to provide the opportunity for both the Aboriginal and the Torres Strait Islander flags to be flown. This is an appropriate form of representation as a matter of social justice for a number of reasons, including the need to differentiate the Aboriginal community from the Torres Strait Islander community and the need to reconcile past injustices of colonisation (not least of which is the long history of Indigenous marginalisation within schools). We are also aware of the ways in which such injustices interlink with the affective domain within schools and are drawn to research which explores the social justice implications of 'care' within this domain (Lynch 2012).

Current context of schooling

The current context of schooling has had a clear impact on the politics of differentiation in many locations. Pasi Sahlberg (2011) suggests that schools are currently subject to a Global Educational Reform Movement–aptly referred to as GERM–which is underpinned by the principles of neo-liberalism. Neo-liberalism, in short, suggests that public institutions are best governed by their ability to succeed in the 'marketplace'. As a consequence they have to be competitive and to market themselves in ways that 'differentiate' themselves from their competitors. The central way in which this happens is through the public representation of a school's academic outcomes, most often typified by the way in which schools respond to their positioning on various league tables. However, schools also seek to market themselves through other means, for example, behaviour policies, uniforms, diverse programs and extracurricular activities. It is not just schools that engage in comparisons but national and local systems too, where governments seek to ensure that they are maximising results within their schools so that they are seen to be competitive with the schooling systems of other nations. For example, it is not uncommon to see headlines in newspapers in Australia and the UK when PISA data, for example, are released such as: 'England's young people near bottom of global league table for basic skills' (Ramesh 2013); 'Pisa tests: NI pupils outshone in global schools comparison' (BBC News Northern Ireland 2013); and 'Billions fail to stop slide in world student rankings' (Ferrari 2013). In order to pressure schools within the system to perform, there have been increasing levels of surveillance and accountability measures introduced, such as the MySchool website in Australia, which is in all but name a league table that compares and ranks schools in relation to their performance on standardised tests (see Hardy 2014).

Significant within Sahlberg's notion of the GERM has been the development of an 'audit culture' (Power 1999) to maximise this accountability. Michael Power has suggested that those located in the UK, and many comparable countries, live in an 'audit society'. He suggests that the 'audit' has come to shape much of social, organisational and political life, and that audits are no longer simply concerned with financial matters. Across many fields, for example, health, social services, public service bureaucracies, higher education and of course school education, vast numbers of people have been employed to monitor and verify the accounts that others provide about the quality of their work. Much has been written about the ways in which schools and teachers have been increasingly regulated through this 'audit culture' (Ball 2012; Lingard 2010; Perryman 2006). Integral to this culture, as indicated above, are various reporting and school assessment frameworks (OFSTED[4]), testing regimes (NAPLAN,[5] PISA[6]) and public representations of data (newspaper league tables, government websites[7]). Whilst these measures have ostensibly been implemented to improve the quality of education experienced by students, it has been noted that they often have 'perverse (or anti-educational) effects' in that they work against such improvement (Lingard & Sellar 2013; Stobart 2008). A narrow focus on raising attainment on testing regimes such as NAPLAN, for example, is seen as undermining school improvement by degrading pedagogy and curriculum to a focus on what is tested. Certainly such a focus is seen as undermining the social learning and citizenship goals of schooling (Cranston et al. 2010; Fullan 2002). We would suggest that the concern with differentiation has also had such perverse effects, and we explore these effects across the chapters in this book.

One aspect of the politics of differentiation is the way it has been employed as a technical solution to a human problem of injustice. Zygmunt Bauman (2004) has variously critiqued the way in which contemporary society has treated human misery as requiring technical solutions, such as placing refugees in off-shore prisons, sending young offenders to boot camps and freezing the welfare payments of parents whose children have been deemed to be truant from school (Cheshire & Zappa 2015; Mills, Renshaw & Zipin 2013). In relation to education, Ball (2013) has suggested that there are three 'technologies' at work in solving problems of student attainment and engagement: market form, management and performativity (pp.48–61). Market form works to position schools as being in competition with each other so as to maximise their market share of high performing students. For this to be an effective technology there has to be the real possibility of failure, in that schools become unviable because they have failed to attract 'high quality' students. Within public sector reforms there has also been a valorisation of the 'manager'. Schools have not been immune to this second 'technology'. In England, for instance, there has been the glorification by both Labour and the Conservatives of 'superheads' on high salaries, who are parachuted into 'failing' schools in order to turn them around (see Judd 1996; Stott 2014). The principal is now expected to ensure that the school is able to drive the new school enterprise in a new world that demands flexibility, adaptability and responsiveness to changing circumstances. This new 'cultural hero' (Ball 2013, p.55) is given a budget and the autonomy to make her or his school the best in the market. However, this autonomy is circumscribed by sets of accountability measures, which frame up the decisions taken by the entrepreneurial principal. Failure to make their school a market success is likely to see their head placed 'on the block' (Thomson 2009). The culture of performativity that is gripping the education system is intertwined with the technologies of management and market reform. Within this system the 'audit culture' referred to earlier in relation to Queensland measures, judges, examines and probes both principals' and teachers' abilities to maximise student outcomes and school enrolments (see Keddie 2013; Lingard & Sellar 2013). Performance is assessed in relation to others' successes (and failures), with those who fail to make the grade placed on notice that their work is going to be even more closely scrutinised.

These technologies appear neutral and seek to take emotion out of decision-making strategies. They work to suggest that the problems facing education, and other human activity, are simply technical ones that can be addressed in a rational and systematic way. However, as suggested by Bauman (2004), they are far from that. They can create significant emotional and material costs for principals/head teachers, teachers and students. Stephen Ball (2013, p.57) refers to the current culture as 'a system of terror' (see also Ball 2003). This system places enormous pressure on principals who in turn place pressure on teachers to ensure that the exam results (often the primary determinant of how schools are judged, although not solely) compare favourably with other schools in the local area. Those working in schools are expected to subscribe to the new agendas, and indeed over time some may come to inhabit the discourses of neo-liberalism quite comfortably and without question. However, for many, this does not always sit comfortably and can lead to frustration, disappointment and disillusionment (Ball 2003; McGregor & Mills 2014). Furthermore, as our work shows, the enactment of policy does not occur seamlessly, universally or cohesively (Braun, Ball, Maguire & Hoskins 2011).

Braun et al. (2011) highlight key contextual factors that impact on how policy is understood and taken up in schools. Drawn from their research in a number of 'ordinary' or 'average' schools in the UK, their work provides a useful four-fold heuristic device for thinking about these factors:

- Situated factors (such as student intake and school history)
- Professional factors (such as teacher values and school ethos)
- Material factors (such as staffing and school budget)
- External factors (such as the pressures and expectations of tests and department policy)

Braun et al. (2011) argue that a school's capacities to cope with and respond to policy are related to these situated, professional, material and external factors. In thinking about policy associated with differentiation–whether at the more structural level of the school or the more student-focused level of the classroom–factors such as student intake, school ethos, school staffing and budgetary constraints matter (see also Keddie 2014b). Certainly, a well-resourced school with a class privileged student demographic and a competitive ethos of high academic achievement will likely approach differentiation differently than a less well-resourced school with a class disadvantaged demographic. Such contextual disparities will likely mean different priorities in terms of differentiation but also different ways of realising policy goals. More advantaged schools will generally be able to meet external policy priorities because their alignment with these priorities does not tend to require a major shift in their core beliefs or dynamics (Braun, Maguire & Ball 2010). In drawing together the analytical themes and findings reported in the chapters of the book we will draw upon Braun et al.'s heuristic to consider how gaps and possibilities for social justice reforms might be pursued through the lens of differentiation.

Context of the study

In 2008 there was a significant outcry at Queensland's results on the National Assessment Plan for Literacy and Numeracy (NAPLAN). These outcomes suggested that Queensland students in the middle primary were performing more poorly than those in all other Australian States and Territories except for the Northern Territory. It was suggested that this could be explained by a steady decline in Queensland students' performances across a number of decades (Masters 2009). In response to these claims, and others (see Masters 2009, pp.12–35), the then Premier of Queensland, Anna Bligh, commissioned the Australian Council for Educational Research (ACER) to undertake a review of education in the State. Out of the findings and recommendations of that review, an audit process was commenced in Queensland and, with it, an accompanying 'Audit Instrument', created by the ACER, containing eight 'dimensions'[8] by which schools could be evaluated and rated. Audits were introduced in 2010, with every government school to be audited at least once every four years, but no more than once in a 12-month period; new schools were not to be audited until the second year of operation. The audits were carried out by 'experienced' school principals who visited a school over a one- to two-day period, depending on the size of the school, and interviewed staff, students and the Parents and Citizens (P & C) Council president. Reports were then provided to the school, which was required to publish the findings for the school community on its website.

The State's main newspaper, *The Courier Mail*, was able to access the results through Freedom of Information legislation, and published the outcomes in a league table form (Chilcott 2012). This led to an outcry by teachers, and the Queensland Teachers' Union placed temporary bans on the process. These were later lifted. What was apparent from *The Courier Mail* table was that of the eight ranked practices, *Differentiated Classroom Learning* was most regularly assessed as being least evident in a school. This played a significant role in informing the direction of our study. The two schools in the study were both enthusiastic about working with us as a means of improving their differentiation practices. We in turn were keen to engage with the agenda of each as a means of understanding how differentiation provoked dialogues and practices regarding social justice concerns of redistribution, recognition and representation.

The study

The two schools in the research, Red Point State High and Crimson State High,[9] are located in the Queensland government sector, which consists of 1,257 schools and education centres. As earlier indicated, these schools were known to us due to their involvement in our teacher education program; they also offered insights into issues facing regional schools. Their location in a regional area of Queensland also meant that they had not been 'over-researched'. As well, the schools offered a number of contrasts, both in their ways of operating and their individual identities. However, as part of the process of gaining permission to conduct research in government schools, one condition was that we not compare the two schools. We have thus avoided such comparison in this book.

Both of these schools received a rating of medium (the report card equivalent of 'could do better') on differentiated learning in the audit. In each case this was the lowest ranking on their school's audit report. After the Teaching and Learning Audit results were made public, the schools engaged with us to expand on the notion of differentiation, and to implement reforms and strategies that took into account the needs of all students in the school. Through the provision of feedback and working closely with the teachers in the two schools, we hope that we have contributed to improved practice there. However, we also hope that the lessons we learnt about differentiation whilst undertaking work there and which form the basis of this book will be of use in other locations.

The study lasted for three years and involved eight week-long visits to each school. We conducted interviews with teachers and a range of other school personnel, for example the principal, deputy principals, Indigenous liaison officers and students. The participants ranged widely in terms of their experience, expertise and length of time at the school. At Red Point High, for example, the principal was new to the school, while the deputy had been at the school over 20 years. At Crimson High, both the principal and deputy had been at the school for over 20 years. The teachers we interviewed spanned across a broad range of curriculum areas with varying duties, expertise and level of seniority, and the ancillary staff also varied in terms of their support roles. As with the broader education community across western contexts, the demographics of the staff were racialised. Almost all of the teachers and senior staff were of White (i.e. Anglo-Australian) heritage. At both schools there was minority representation but this tended to be limited to the ancillary staff (e.g. both schools employed a small number of Indigenous staff). Both schools were also situated in a locale that was highly racialised. The conservative regional centre that these schools served still suffered from the remnants of its long and troubled colonial past with the Indigenous community remaining highly disadvantaged economically and socially. We explore some of these issues of staffing and representation further in the subsequent chapters as they are relevant to the themes in the book.

Most of the participants were interviewed multiple times. The interviews were loosely structured around a series of focus prompts that sought to explore each participant's role at the school, their thoughts about the school and its students, their understandings of social justice in general, and of differentiation more specifically, and their thoughts on the key enablers and constraints to creating classrooms that were conducive to *all* students receiving a high quality education. We also conducted classroom observations and ran workshops, with teachers participating in the study for feedback on our findings. In this book we principally draw on interview data and data collected from teachers during workshops. Our analytical approach to these data broadly draws on Fraser's three-dimensional framework explained above. Underpinning our analytic for each chapter is our concern with social justice and how particular constructions of differentiation address or further entrench relations of maldistribution, misrecognition and misrepresentation. Further explanation of how these tools are used analytically is explored in greater depth in each chapter to tease out the particularities of the politics of differentiation in relation to pedagogy, curriculum, extracurricular programs and how the schools navigate the demands of the current policy context.

In relation to our representation of the marginalised voices in this book, we want to acknowledge our own positionality as White middle class and privileged researchers. Our attempts to provide insight into marginality and disadvantage are thus mindful of the necessity to decentre this privilege and the imperialist or paternalistic representations that such privilege may produce (see Moreton-Robinson 1998). We do this through our critical approach and, in particular, through the social justice framings Fraser's work offers.

The schools

The following introduces the two schools featured in this book, Red Point High and Crimson High, drawing upon Braun et al.'s (2011) heuristic device of contextual factors: Situated, Professional, Material and External.

Red Point

Situated: Red Point High was established in the late 1950s and expanded to become one of the largest high schools in Queensland. The school had a history of being a 'traditional' school, and pride in traditions of academic excellence and high expectations in relation to behaviour, attendance and academic effort were expressed to us. At the time of our visit it catered to approximately 1,500 students who were generally drawn from the local area and were from middle class backgrounds–it had a small, but substantial, for a metropolitan school, Indigenous population (6 per cent) and a small percentage of students whose language background was other than English (4 per cent), but students were predominantly of Anglo-Australian heritage. Due to the school's reputation as a 'good' school, it had a management enrolment plan to restrict student numbers to approximately 1,500. The school website suggests that it has the leading music program in the region, for which students have to audition. This facilitates high achieving 'out of catchment area' students being able to enrol in the school.

Professional: Red Point has a strong reputation for academic excellence and, especially during our early visits to the school, indicated a pride in its private school image and high standards of behaviour. The school's principal was new to the school in the first year of our visit, and the previous principal had only been at the school for three years. However, the school reputation and school ethos was entrenched amongst the staff, many of whom had been at the school for very long periods of time. Within the leadership team there were concerns about developing intercultural and international awareness, and preparing students for global as well as Australian citizenship. In relation to ethos, the school articulated a need for a safe and caring environment within which students and staff were expected to demonstrate values related to such attributes as co-operation and respect. Whilst Red Point High provides a comprehensive curriculum, there was some curriculum differentiation in the senior years to provide students with academic and vocational pathways. Attendance of students and teachers at the school was better than the state average, suggesting that the climate in the school was positive for both teachers and students. This was supported by the results of a centrally designed and administered satisfaction survey of students, parents and teachers.

Material: The school was well resourced in terms of staffing. For example, approximately 25 per cent of staff were employed in a non-teaching capacity with the focus being on supporting teachers and students. For example, this included a full-time Aboriginal and Torres Strait Islander Community Education Counsellor, whose responsibility was to provide pastoral care and support, and advocacy for Indigenous students within the school community, and a School Based Youth Health Nurse four days a week to support both student and teacher wellbeing.

External: Engagement with external factors appeared to be embraced by senior figures in the school. External measures of school effectiveness, for example, their score on the Queensland Teaching and Learning Audit on differentiation, prompted their professional development focus on differentiation of learning. This commitment to teacher professional development was demonstrated by the willingness of the school to provide teacher relief for the teachers in our study to spend time in planning workshops with us. Teachers also spoke of their opportunities for professional development, including flights to the State's capital Brisbane to attend workshops with Carol Tomlinson, an international advocate for pedagogical differentiation (see Chapter 2). The teachers we interviewed demonstrated a commitment to the notion of the school as a caring place where traditional values were upheld and to pursuing academic excellence. However, how the school responded to external factors was contentious. For instance, there were some teachers who expressed concerns about 'rubbish' students being enrolled in the school whilst there were some teachers who were critical of the selectivity and management practices of the school. Some teachers also suggested that the external factors of a focus on narrow outcomes, policy and curriculum expectations, external audits and the like were leading to greater surveillance within the school and a silencing of dissent.

Crimson

Situated: Crimson High opened in the late 1970s. It is located in the same city as Red Point High. However, its student population comes from poorer backgrounds than many of those at Red Point. It is proud of its tradition of serving some of the most marginalised young people in the city. It has approximately 2,000 students and a large Indigenous population (19 per cent). The school has taken on the responsibility of educating young Indigenous people from a nearby Island community after their high school program was closed down. It is worth noting that this island originally served as a reserve to isolate Indigenous people who were deemed 'disruptive' or unlawful. Approximately 11 per cent of students at the school speak a language other than English at home. Over 40 cultural groups are represented in the student cohort.

Professional: Crimson High prides itself on being a 'school for all'. The leadership team was very well established, with the principal having been at the school for almost 30 years and the senior deputy over 20 years. This team had been central to creating this vision for the school. The school had a highly valued Indigenous cultural program; during our research period the school attained accreditation as an 'International School'; it also runs music and sporting excellence programs.

Reflective of the international focus of the school and its commitment to being a socially inclusive school, it notes that relationships within the whole school community are underpinned by the tenets of the United Nations Universal Declaration of Human Rights. Due to the size of the school it is able to offer a broad range of curricula and extracurricular programs. For example, in the Senior School, students could choose from over 60 academic and vocational subjects. The school has specialist Excellence Programs in Music and in over 10 different sports. Attendance of students at the school was slightly under the state average, although Indigenous student attendance was higher than the state average for Indigenous attendance. Staff attendance was average. Nevertheless, these data, when read alongside the positive results of the satisfaction survey completed by students, parents and teachers, would seem to reinforce the positive views we as a research team felt about the climate of the school.

Material: As with Red Point High, the school had good staff resources with it also having approximately 25 per cent non-teaching support staff. Amongst these support staff was a student wellbeing team that had the responsibility for delivering a range of proactive programs and working with individual students on matters related to their study but also to those related to their emotional and physical needs. During our time at the school an 'Engagement Team' was created. This consisted of five non-teaching staff whose role was to build relationships between the school and families, through home visits, to ensure that those who had difficulties in attending school on a regular basis were supported. The school also had five Indigenous staff members who worked closely with students, their families and the community.

External: Crimson High, again like Red Point High, engaged with external indicators of success enthusiastically. These included those set through departmental priorities and those that gave them broad recognition within the local, national and international community (marketplace). As with Red Point High, and the vast majority of schools' scores on the Queensland Teaching and Learning Audit, they were only average on the 'Classroom differentiation' item. The school did appear to take a critical approach to reform in terms of discerning and shaping their responses to policy. This could be attributed to the stability, confidence and strength of the leadership team at the school built over many years. This school took a broad approach to professional development around issues of pedagogy. They welcomed our visit as a means of receiving feedback on what was working well and how classroom practice could be improved. This was also supported through teacher relief to participate in the study. As part of its engagement with external factors, the school was very busy! For example, during the time of the study, the school had participated in and won major awards in the fields of Aboriginal and Torres Strait Islander education, literacy and numeracy and multiculturalism. It was also accredited by a number of other bodies to become, for example, a Microsoft Innovative Pathfinder school; an Asian Learning Centre; Queensland Minerals and Energy Academy Gateway School; and the Habits of Mind International Learning Community of Excellence. Teachers appeared supportive, if at times overworked, in relation to the pressures created by the school's responses to external factors.

Chapter outlines

In this introductory chapter of the book we have highlighted some of the complexities and contentions surrounding schools and their engagement with a politics of differentiation. We have pointed out how Nancy Fraser's conceptualisation of social justice provides a foundation for thinking through issues of injustice that impact upon such differentiation. We then situated our study within a set of politics that are shaping the context of schooling, also indicating how they were having a direct impact upon our case study schools. We then indicated the research parameters of the study upon which this book is based and described the focus schools of our research.

In Chapter 2 we explore the notion of 'pedagogical differentiation', as advocated by Tomlinson (1995; 1999; 2008), and the ways in which such differentiation was understood by teachers at Red Point High. It was this form of differentiation that the Teaching and Learning Audit identified as having been absent in the majority of Queensland government school classrooms. Whilst providing a critique of differentiated pedagogy as instantiated in the practices of the teachers at Red Point High, and noting its problematic policy location as an audit and accountability instrument to govern teachers' practices, we argue that a focus on differentiation can contribute to more socially just classrooms when accompanied by a commitment to valuing cultural differences.

In Chapter 3 we explore how the discourse of teacher expectations relates to the politics of differentiation at Red Point High. Teachers often invoked the term 'high expectations' as a very positive aspect of the school's culture; however, our analysis of the interviews shows that the meaning of high expectations was far from uniform. Rather than being an invitation to provide the highest quality schooling to all students who might enrol at Red Point High, it became a means of maintaining the reputation of the school itself and resisting attempts to broaden the diversity of students at the school. For particular teachers, for example, the Indigenous worker and the welfare officer, the use of the term 'high expectations' was an urgent call to address the needs of more marginalised students at Red Point High. Likewise the principal, Phil, deployed high expectations as a critical lens to examine teaching in the lower-streamed classes and challenge teachers to lift the quality of teaching offered to students most in need of support. As with the notion of differentiated pedagogy (Chapter 2), high expectations could be deployed to close down options for productive dialogue about social justice or open up possibilities for dealing proactively with the more marginalised members of the school community.

In Chapter 4 we foreground the emotional dimensions of differentiated teaching through an analysis of the discourses of care and solidarity at Red Point High, to counter the 'eerie absence' of care mentioned in the previous chapter in relation to the technical and reductionist framings of quality teaching (Masters 2009; McKinsey 2007). In contrast to this technical framing of teaching, we highlight the stories of concern and worry that teachers express for specific groups of students as well as individuals in their classrooms, their accounts of emotionally charged experiences with students and the intense care they offer to specific students. We draw upon interviews with students at Red Point High, various classroom teachers, as well as the Welfare Officer, the Deputy Principal and Principal. Our interviews included quite intense stories of personal investment by particular teachers in trying to negotiate new identities for the students and mediating new relationships between the students, the school and their parents. The stories in this chapter will be familiar to many who work in schools. What we offer in this chapter is a way of interpreting such stories in terms of how social justice is constrained and limited through particular understandings of care, and how we might see justice more broadly in relation to care and differentiation.

Chapter 5 takes up the tensions of curriculum, how it is defined, whose interests are represented and the politics of its construction. We shift the focus from teacher accountability to consider the role of curriculum in terms of its long-term impact on student learning. We explore the notion of a *school for all*–a key marker at Crimson High–to investigate the ways in which this school pursues a social justice agenda through its curriculum. Specifically, we focus on the music curriculum as an example of how a highly differentiated curriculum enables student agency. We acknowledge the complexity of competing approaches; on the one hand providing 'hooks' to engage students and open opportunities and, on the other, ensuring that differentiated pathways do not consign students to travel through corridors to nowhere. We discuss the implications for schools in terms of defining what social justice means in their specific context, and how this might inform their own curriculum. We also incorporate the voices of students who are otherwise struggling with academic studies to provide insights into the impact of a differentiated curriculum on their school experiences.

The focus in Chapter 6 is on the politics of differentiation, culture and Indigeneity at Crimson High. We examine the school's concerns about Indigenous disadvantage and the various approaches undertaken to address this. We highlight how cultural recognition is an important organising principle in struggles for justice but also how it can undermine justice through reifying cultural difference as other and deficit. Like the earlier chapters, the politics represented in this chapter bring to light the complexities of differentiation and an absence of consistency in relation to how such differentiation might best be approached. Also consistent with the earlier chapters, our intention here is to highlight possibilities for working in more socially just ways. The key argument in this chapter is that such possibilities are enabled by educators being critically aware of how they construct race and use it as an organising principle in their work. This awareness is central to moving beyond the cultural essentialism that tends to predominate within Indigenous education–where cultural reductionism homogenises Indigeneity within and against a dominant White norm. In particular, we argue the imperative of educators understanding culture as an aspect of negotiated social practice rather than a fixed entity. With reference to a specific approach at the school designed predominantly for Indigenous male students–to foster intercultural awareness and respect through sport–we highlight ways in which notions of culturalism and racial incommensurability might be disrupted.

In the final chapter we draw together the key findings of the book and provide further insight into how differentiation might be framed within schools to better align with social justice goals. We draw here on Braun et al.'s (2010) heuristic device (introduced in Chapter 1) to re-examine the significance that particular contextual factors at Red Point and Crimson played in relation to matters of differentiation for social justice. With reference to the major themes threaded through the book around pedagogy, curriculum, expectations, care and extra-curricular practices, we highlight some of the *situated* (e.g. student intake and school history); *professional* (e.g. teacher values and school ethos); *material* (e.g. staffing and school budget) and *external* (e.g. the pressures and expectations of tests and department policy) factors that both enabled and constrained the pursuit of economic, cultural and political justice at both schools. This chapter also draws out threads associated with leadership that run through our accounts of each school–recognising the significance of school leadership in powerfully shaping the politics of differentiation in each of the schools in relation to pursuing a socially just approach to student differentiation. We conclude the chapter with a set of provocations based on the book's primary insights with the aim of proliferating new lines of thought and enquiry.

Notes

1 See for example http://www.creativespirits.info/aboriginalculture/spirituality/welcome-to-country-acknowledgement-of-country#axzz3h9EKZtj9.
2 See https://www.gov.uk/pupil-premium-information-for-schools-and-alternative-provision-settings.
3 See http://www.humanservices.gov.au/customer/services/centrelink/abstudy.
4 Office for Standards in Education, Children's Services and Skills, School Inspection Framework, http://www.ofsted.gov.uk/resources/framework-for-school-inspection.
5 National Assessment Plan–Literacy and Numeracy. National annual standardised tests of years 3, 5, 7 and 9 students.
6 Programme for International Student Assessment. International tests, sponsored by the OECD, that seek to evaluate education systems worldwide. They are conducted every three years and assess 15-year-olds' competencies in: reading, mathematics and science. See http://www.oecd.org/pisa/.
7 The My School website, http://www.myschool.edu.au/, is sponsored by the Australian Curriculum, Assessment and Reporting Authority (ACARA), and provides information about every school in Australia including results on NAPLAN.
8 These include: An Explicit Improvement Agenda; Analysis and Discussion of Data; A Culture that Promotes Learning; Targeted Use of School Resources; An Expert Teaching Team; Systematic Curriculum Delivery; Differentiated Classroom Learning and Effective Teaching Practices (Master, 2010).
9 Pseudonyms are used for all places and people related to the case study.

References

Amin, R, Browne, DC, Jamir AMA, & Sato, TMA 2006, A study of an alternative school for pregnant and/or parenting teens: Quantitative and qualitative evidence. *Child and Adolescent Social Work Journal*, Vol. 23, no. 2, pp. 172–195.

Ball, S 2003, 'The teacher's soul and the terrors of performativity', *Journal of Education Policy*, Vol. 18, no. 2, pp. 215–228.

Ball, S 2012, *Global education Inc.: New policy networks and the neo-liberal imaginary*, Routledge, London.

Ball, S 2013, *The education debate* 2nd edn, Policy Press, Bristol.

Barber, M & Mourshed, M 2007, *How the world's best performing school systems come out on top*, McKinsey & Company, New York.

Baroutsis, A, McGregor, G, Mills, M 2015, 'Pedagogic voice: Student voice in teaching and engagement pedagogies', *Pedagogy, Culture and Society*, doi: 10.1080/14681366.2015.1087044

Baroutsis, A, Mills, M, McGregor, G, te Riele, K, & Hayes, D 2016, 'Student voice and the community forum: Finding ways of "being heard" at an alternative school for disenfranchised young people', *British Educational Research Journal*, accepted 22 July, 2015.

Bauman, Z 2004, *Wasted lives: Modernity and its outcasts*, Oxford, Polity Press.

Black, R 2011, 'Student participation and disadvantage: limitations in policy and practice', *Journal of Youth Studies*, Vol. 14, no. 4, pp. 463–474.

Bragg, S 2007, '"Student voice" and governmentality: The production of enterprising subjects?', *Discourse: Studies in the Cultural Politics of Education*, Vol. 28, no. 3, pp. 343–358.

Braun, A, Ball, SJ, Maguire, M, & Hoskins, K 2011, 'Taking context seriously: Towards explaining policy enactments in the Secondary School', *Discourse: Studies in the Cultural Politics of Education*, Vol. 32, no. 4, pp. 585–596.

Braun, A, Maguire, M, & Ball, SJ 2010, 'Policy enactments in the UK Secondary School: Examining policy, practice and school positioning', *Journal of Education Policy*, Vol. 25, no. 4, pp. 547–560.

Carswell, SB, Hanlon, TE, O'Grady, KE, Watts, AM, & Pothong, P 2009, 'A preventive intervention program for urban African American youth attending an alternative education program: Background, implementation, and feasibility', *Education and Treatment of Children*, Vol. 32, no. 3, pp. 445–469.

Cheshire, L, & Zappia, G 2015, 'Destination dumping ground: The convergence of "unwanted" populations in disadvantaged city areas', *Urban Studies*, doi: 10.1177/0042098015587241

Chilcott, T 2012, 'Report card: How your school stacks up', *The Courier-Mail*, 28 January, Available from: http://www.couriermail.com.au. [7 March 2013].

Connell, RW 1994, 'Poverty and education', *Harvard Educational Review*, Vol. 64, no. 2, pp. 125–149.

Cranston N, Mulford B, Keating J, et al 2010, 'Primary school principals and the purposes of schooling in Australia', *Journal of Educational Administration*, Vol. 48, no. 4, pp. 517–539.

Department of Education, Employment and Workplace Relations (DEEWR) 2011, *7.5 million to help increase Indigenous teacher numbers*, Government of Australia. Available from: http://ministers.deewr.gov.au. [23 March 2012].

Department of Education and Training 2011, *Embedding Aboriginal and Torres Strait Islander perspectives: A guide for school learning communities*, State Government of Queensland. Available from: http://indigenous.education.qld.gov.au. [22 December 2014].

Everest, C 2003, 'Differentiation, the new monster in education: Differentiation is just another pressure meted out by managers', *The Guardian*, 18 February, Available from: https://www.theguardian.com/education/2003/feb/18/further education.uk4. [14 January 2016].

Ferrari, J 2013. 'Billions fail to stop slide in world student rankings', *The Australian*, 4 December. Available from: http://theaustralian.com.au. [4 December 2015]

Fielding, M 2004a, '" New wave" student voice and the renewal of civic society', *London Review of Education*, Vol. 2, no. 3, pp. 197–297.

Fielding, M 2004b, 'Transformative approaches to student voice: Theoretical underpinnings, recalcitrant realities', *British Educational Research Journal*, Vol. 30, no. 2, pp. 295–311.

Fraser, N 1997, *Justice interruptus: Critical reflections on the 'postsocialist' condition*, Routledge, New York.

Fraser, N 2009, *Scales of justice: Reimagining political space in a globalizing world*, Columbia University Press, New York.

Fullan, M 2002, 'The change leader', *Educational Leadership*, Vol. 59, no. 8, pp. 16–21.

Gable, A & Lingard, B (2015). NAPLAN data: A new policy assemblage and mode of governance in Australian schooling. *Policy Studies*, DOI:10.1080/01442872.2015.1115830.

Gonski, D., Boston, K, Greiner, K, Lawrence, C, Scales, B, & Tannock, P. (2011). *Review of Funding for Schooling: Final Report.* Australian Government. Available at https://docs.education.gov.au/system/files/doc/other/review-of-funding-for-schooling-final-report-dec-2011.pdf

Gowlett, C. Keddie, A., Mills, M. Renshaw, P. Geelan, D., Monk, S. and Christie, P. (2014). 'Using Butler to understand the multiplicity and variability of curriculum policy reception', *Journal of Education Policy*, Vol. 30, no. 2, pp. 149–164.

Hardy, I 2014, 'A logic of enumeration: The nature and effects of national literacy and numeracy testing in Australia', *Journal of Education Policy*, Vol. 30, no. 3, pp. 335–362.

Judd, J 1996, 'Super heads' to rescue schools: Blair speech today will set out his plans for making education Labour's leading priority', *The Independent*, 16 December. Available from: http://www.independent.co.uk [15 Sept 2014].

Keddie, A 2012a, *Educating for diversity and social justice*, Routledge, New York.

Keddie, A 2012b, 'Schooling and social justice through the lenses of Nancy Fraser', *Critical Studies in Education*, Vol. 53, no. 3, pp. 263–279.

Keddie, A 2013a, 'Thriving amid the performative demands of the contemporary audit culture: A matter of school context', *Journal of Education Policy*, Vol. 8, no. 6, pp. 750–766.

Kenway, J 2013b, 'Challenging inequality in Australian schools: Gonski and beyond', *Discourse: Studies in the Cultural Politics of Education*, Vol. 34, no. 2, pp. 286–308.

Keddie, A 2014a, 'Student voice and teacher accountability: Possibilities and problematics', *Pedagogy, Culture and Society*, Vol. 23, no. 2, pp. 225–244.

Keddie, A 2014b, '"It's like Spiderman . . . with great power comes great responsibility": School autonomy and the audit culture', *School Leadership and Management*, Vol. 34, no. 5, pp. 502–517.

Ladson-Billings, G 1995, 'Toward a theory of culturally relevant pedagogy', *American Educational Research Journal*, Vol. 32, no. 3, pp. 465–491.

Lingard, B 2010, 'Policy borrowing, policy learning: Testing times in Australian schooling', *Critical Studies in Education*, Vol. 51, no. 2, pp. 129–147.

Lingard, B, & Sellar, S 2013, '"Catalyst data": Perverse systemic effects of audit and accountability in Australian schooling', *Journal of Education Policy*, Vol. 28, no. 5, pp. 634–656.

Lynch, K 2012, 'Affective equality as a key issue of justice: A comment on Fraser's 3-dimensional framework', *Social Justice Series*, Vol. 12, no. 3, pp. 45–64.

Masters, G 2009, *A Shared Challenge: improving literacy, numeracy and science learning in Queensland primary schools*, The Australian Council for Educational Research, Melbourne.

McGregor, G & Mills, M 2014, 'Teaching in the "Margins": The politics of teachers' work in alternative schools', *British Journal of Sociology of Education*, Vol. 35, no. 1, pp. 1–18.Mills, C & Gale, T 2010, *Schooling in disadvantaged communities*, Springer, New York.

Mills, M & McGregor, G 2014, *Re-engaging young people in education: Learning from alternative schools*, Routledge, London.

Mills, M, Renshaw, P, & Zipin, L 2013, 'Alternative education provision: A dumping ground for "wasted lives" or a challenge to the mainstream?', *Social Alternatives*, Vol. 32, no. 2, pp. 13–18.

Ministerial Council on Education, Employment, Training and Youth Affairs (MCEETYA) 2008, *Melbourne Declaration on the Educational Goals for Young Australians*, The State Government of Victoria. Available from: https://www.curriculum.edu.au [22 December 2014].

Mitra, DL 2009, 'Collaborating with students: Building youth-adult partnerships in schools', *American Journal of Education*, Vol. 115, no. 3, pp. 407–436.

Moreton-Robinson, A 1998, 'When the object speaks, a postcolonial encounter: Anthropological representations and Aboriginal women's self-presentations', *Discourse: Studies in the Cultural Politics of Education*, Vol. 19, no. 3, pp. 275–289.

Perryman, J 2006, 'Panoptic performativity and school inspection regimes: Disciplinary mechanisms and life under special measures', *Journal of Education Policy*, Vol. 21, no. 2, pp. 147–161.

'Pisa tests: NI pupils outshone in global schools comparison', *BBC News Northern Ireland* 3 December. Available from: http://www.bbc.com [12 January 2014].

Power, M 1999, *The audit society: Rituals of verification*, Oxford University Press, Oxford.

Ramesh, R 2013, 'England's young people near bottom of global league table for basic skills', *Guardian*, 8 October. Available from: http://www.theguardian.com [13 January 2014].

Rudduck, J & Fielding, M 2006, 'Student voice and the perils of popularity', *Educational Review*, Vol. 58, no. 2, pp. 219–231.

Sahlberg, P 2011, *Finnish lessons: What can the World learn from educational change in Finland?*, Teachers College Press, New York.

Sarra, C 2003, 'Cherbourg State School, strong and smart', *What Works Program: Improving Outcomes for Indigenous Students*. Available from: http://www.whatworks.edu.au. [10 March 2011].

Stobart, G 2008, *Testing times: The uses and abuses of assessment*, Routledge, New York.

Stott, M 2014, 'Suffolk: "Super heads" to rescue failing schools after Suffolk County Council joins Talented Leaders scheme', *East Anglian Daily Times*, 10 September. Available from: [15 September 2014].

Thomson, P 2009, *School leadership: Heads on the block*, Routledge, London.

Tomlinson, C 1995, 'Deciding to differentiate instruction in the middle school: One school's journey', *Gifted Child Quarterly*, Vol. 39, no. 2, pp. 77–114.

Tomlinson, C 1999, 'Mapping a route toward differentiated instruction', *Educational Leadership*, Vol. 57, no. 1, pp. 12–16.

Tomlinson, CA 2008, 'Goals of differentiation', *Educational Leadership*, Vol. 66, no. 3, pp. 26–30.

Zipin, L, Sellar, S, & Hattam, R 2012, 'Countering and exceeding "capital": A "funds of knowledge" approach to re-imagining community', *Discourse: Studies in the Cultural Politics of Education*, Vol. 33, no. 2, pp. 179–192.

2 A politics of differentiation and pedagogy

In this chapter we are concerned with pedagogical differentiation, that is, how teachers structure their classrooms and interact with students so as to meet their diverse needs. Advocacy for differentiation has been evident and a source of concern in a number of locations. For example, the *Times Education Supplement* (Dixie 2011) provides advice to new teachers in England on how to differentiate their classrooms, and in Australia the NSW Department of Education and Communities website (2016) advocates curriculum differentiation for 'gifted students'. An article in the UK *Guardian* in 2003, headlined 'Differentiation, the new monster in education–Differentiation is just another pressure meted out by managers', captures the frustration of some teachers who feel that this policy is impacting negatively on their classroom practice (Everest 2003). In Queensland, where the case studies are located, differentiation was mandated through an audit of teaching and learning. Publication of data on these audits indicated that the implementation of 'differentiation' was problematic for teachers. We would suggest that this may well be the case in many locations.

Our focus in this chapter is on how the mandate to differentiate was interpreted by teachers and influenced their practices at Red Point High. The principal at Red Point High, Phil, had been a member of one of the Teaching and Learning Audit teams mentioned in Chapter 1 prior to taking up his position at the school. He noted this about the Queensland schools he had visited as part of the audit process:

> From previous experiences working around the State and looking at Teaching and Learning Audits and the particular area around differentiation . . . there's been an overwhelming recognition that differentiation is not done well in school.

Part of the problem appears to be that differentiation has been variously conceived. At one level it can be seen in terms of a system, whereby there are different types of schools designed for different types of students. Current policy initiatives in a range of locations include selective academic academies and high schools where excellence and high performance are claimed to be maximised. The negative effects of this differentiated and selective system on children from low socio-economic and particular ethnic and racial communities have been well documented (see Ball 2012;Coldron, Cripps & Shipton 2010; Connell 1993; Laitsch 2013). Underlying an approach that groups students according to ability is an assumption that 'an intellectually homogeneous student body fosters the development of talent and enhances efficient teaching, thus improving the quality of educational outcomes' (OECD 2005, p.48).

This assumption also underpins much of the differentiation currently occurring at the school level. Within schools, differentiation is most obvious in terms of distinctions made between academic and vocational programs (see Chapter 5). Other examples may be 'gifted and talented' programs, 'special education' classes or the streaming of classes according to student test results or behaviour (see for example, Kronborg & Plunkett 2008; Noble 2004; see also Chapter 3). However, differentiation can also occur at a class level; this usually involves splitting the class into small groups, assigning individual learning activities or modifying curriculum materials based on perceived ability. In this sense, it is perhaps not distinct from other forms of differentiation that separate students on the basis of 'abilities'. However, within-class differentiation can also entail a recognition of the different knowledges that various students bring to the classroom, their differing skills and their diverse interests and circumstances, and responding in ways that value these differences and use them to engage students in the work of the classroom, all of which have been seen as critical to ensuring that students marginalised by poverty and cultural discrimination are able to access school curricula (Gonzalez, Moll & Amanti 2005; Zipin et al. 2012). Seen in this light, differentiation is very much concerned with addressing economic and cultural injustices (Fraser 1997; 2009).

The form of differentiation that we are concerned with in this chapter is 'pedagogical differentiation', or in US terms, 'instructional differentiation'. It is this form of differentiation that most aligns with that advocated within Queensland's *Teaching and Learning School Improvement Framework* (Masters 2010). It is perhaps no surprise that the audit of schools found little evidence of differentiation, as Subban (2006, p.938) has indicated: 'Uniformity, rather than attending to diversity, dominates the culture of many contemporary classrooms'. We thus argue that if differentiation is to help contribute to more socially just classrooms, the primary importance of valuing difference per se has to be acknowledged.

In the chapter we explore the ways in which some of the Red Point High teachers engaged with the audit requirement to differentiate their classrooms. We explore these issues through the voices of 10 of the 20 school personnel interviewed at Red Point: the principal, 'Phil', and key teachers, 'Lucy' (head of drama), 'Florence' (head of English), 'Mary' (drama teacher) and 'Sonia' (social science, literacy and numeracy teacher), and other teachers ('Aisha', 'Bianca' and 'Cherie', 'Jen' and 'Diane'). These voices appear here because they encapsulate the key issues that seemed to be significant at the school in relation to differentiation to support enhanced student learning: issues of grouping and individualisation and streaming in relation to pedagogical differentiation and issues of individualisation in relation to assessment. The salience of these issues generated our emphasis in relation to analysing the interview data in terms of identifying the key and emerging themes informed by the literature. Given our concerns with the reportedly 'perverse' effects of the audit culture in relation to constraining pedagogical differentiation within contemporary schools, our analysis then turned to a focus on how this culture intersected with teachers' concerns about their classroom practices in relation to differentiation.

Data from the school indicated that teachers had not been provided with a consistent message about what differentiation meant, nor adequate support for implementing this policy requirement; and of more concern, they experienced the audit requirements as being under increased surveillance from above. Furthermore, other reforms, notably the national reform to introduce the Australian Curriculum and a set of teaching support materials produced at the state level, Curriculum into the Classroom (C2C), competed with differentiation for teachers' attention and were interpreted by teachers to be at odds with the intent of differentiation. However, we suggest that some spaces were opened up by the Teaching and Learning Audit, perhaps ironically given many of the 'perverse effects' generated by an audit culture, that could potentially support the pursuit of a social justice agenda in the school (Apple 2005; Grek et al. 2009; Keddie et al. 2011; Lingard & Sellar 2013). We do not want to trivialise the impacts of an audit culture upon those working and studying in schools, but in looking for spaces, opportunities and points of resistance within this culture we hope to reveal new ways for pursuing a social justice agenda within the contemporary policy framework. Data from this school add support to the notion that differentiation is a complex concept which is not easy to shift from a policy to a classroom context, and which requires more careful explication at the policy level and also more support for teachers to enact.

Mandating pedagogical differentiation

The intention of the Queensland Teaching and Learning Audit was to provide 'quality feedback' and 'collect a range of data and information about school practices, programs and procedures in the area of teaching and learning . . . [a]s part of an initiative to improve student learning . . .'.[1] External audits can be useful in helping schools identify their achievements as well as their challenges. They can thus provide an opportunity to reflect on school-based management and practices that are working to benefit student learning and support teachers in this work. Therefore the data that are gathered are potentially valuable in terms of how they can be used to initiate staff conversations and guide professional development at a school level. However, it could be argued that the assigned rating of 'outstanding', 'high', 'medium' or 'low' against each of the eight criteria introduced a ranking component, which, together with the online public release of schools' results, worked against the intention of the audit. Additionally, the results of an external audit may not necessarily align with the school's own perceptions of its performance in delivering educational opportunities to its students. The political agenda that drives the audit process therefore can sit uncomfortably with staff who may feel that it does not take into account other contextual factors. This point was taken up at Red Point High, where the principal, Phil, commented that not all staff would share the rating of 'medium' for the school's performance in differentiated classroom learning, and that some ratings could breed complacency:

> I think that's . . . the challenge . . . particularly because the school gets such good outcomes, you know, the school gets great results, so, I mean a lot of the teachers could sit back and say, 'Well, why should we change [when] we're getting great results'.

The difficulty for the principal was not confined to convincing teachers of the need for a different way of doing things; the dilemma carried over into other areas that impacted on the school's reputation. Phil explained how he perceived the school's relationship with the broader community:

> There are parents that came here, so regardless of where they happen to live now, whether they live out in other areas where there [are] other high schools, they will still want to send their kids here.

The relationships between Red Point High and the community had been cultivated over several generations and some teachers at this school expressed an awareness that within the broader community there was a strong understanding that the school focuses on high academic achievement. In the following extract Phil explained that the school's enrolment plan helped to maintain the school's standing and that this too helped to make many teachers unwilling to change their practices:

> The enrolment management plan . . . effectively brings in better clientele to the school. So we're getting a significant proportion of good kids, brighter kids, into the school in the first place and so the teachers have got to know what they're doing in terms of value-adding. . . . And that was a bit of an eye opener for the teachers 'cause they were a bit blown away to see that the relative gain is actually not really good here, 'cause the kids [who] are coming are coming in so bright, and it is harder to get that improvement at that top end. So, I think that's probably one of the biggest challenges around the nature of this school . . . that there [are] traditional ways that things have been done and to convince people that there are better ways to teach.

The idea of 'value-adding' and 'relative-gain' is a particular way of thinking about how audits can be used within a school. Whilst the notion of 'value added' is not uncontested (see Reynolds & Teddlie 2002), the principal's main concern was to provide professional development to teachers. Because of the concern with differentiation, this professional development centred on the extensive work of Carol Tomlinson in relation to teacher classroom practice.

Carol Tomlinson has been one of the most ardent supporters of 'instructional differentiation' and was regularly cited by teachers we interviewed. Her work on differentiation spans from the mid-1990s to the present (see for example, 1995; 1999; 2000; 2005; 2008). There is much to support in Tomlinson's work in relation to promoting socially just classrooms. She argues that differentiation entails providing all students with challenging and safe and supportive classrooms where there is focus on disciplinary knowledges, where teachers employ a range of methods, including whole class, small group and individual arrangements, and where 'teachers use time, space, materials, and instructional strategies in flexible ways to address varied learner needs' (Tomlinson 2005, p.263). She also argues that classrooms need to be communities where students have their voices heard. In outlining the goals of differentiation, Tomlinson (2008) claims that teachers need to build trust in the classroom, to create an environment where the students care about the work that they are expected to undertake because it is meaningful to them and connected to their worlds. She also articulates what could be seen as a form of political justice in her concern with democratic classrooms, through her advocacy of student voice as a goal of differentiation. According to Subban (2006, p.941), in differentiated classrooms, 'teachers should find ways to engage students, by tapping into what interests students, and by involving students in the daily running of the classroom'.

To differentiate in the ways that Tomlinson and others articulate, it becomes apparent that teachers need to know and understand their students. This includes having an understanding of the various injustices they may experience in their lives both inside and outside the school grounds. Subban (2006), in a wide ranging literature review of 'differentiated instruction', argued that contemporary classrooms characterised by diversity on a number of levels, for example, social, cultural and intellectual, require forms of pedagogy that can engage students in classwork. As such she contends that the curriculum has to be connected to their lives. This, Subban (2006, p.941) indicates, emphasising the work of Tomlinson (2005), requires teachers to know their students, including their 'cultural links'. Reflecting the arguments related to pedagogical models such as the productive pedagogies framework (Hayes et al. 2006) that stressed the need for classrooms where difference was valued within a learning community, she claims that 'differentiated instruction supports the classroom as a community, accommodating difference and sameness'. Ginsberg (2005) argues that respecting cultural diversity and drawing upon students' cultural knowledges also increases the motivation of students who have perhaps switched off from school. We regarded the teachers' reference to Tomlinson's ideas, therefore, as potentially progressive and indicative of heightened interest in students themselves, and their families and communities.

One issue that regularly raised its head in connection with differentiation is its relationship with assessment, as indicated in the case study data below. There is some sense that whilst classrooms may take into account differences amongst learners, assessment should not be differentiated. The arguments are many. They include, for instance, that grades across a year level and subject are only meaningful if all students have undertaken the same task, that having different tasks for different students will not challenge all students intellectually; that different expectations of students reinforces the deficit construction of some, usually marginalised, students; and that students will acquire a false sense of their abilities. However, there are arguments that suggest that high quality assessment practice and differentiation are not incompatible (see for example, McTighe & Brown 2005; Moon 2005; Tomlinson 2005). Various proponents of differentiation have outlined the synergies between the two. For example, Moon argues that three of the key principles of differentiation are that learning has to be active, involve high expectations (with appropriate scaffolding) and that it should occur in a social context (Moon 2005, p.231). These are all characteristics of high quality 'authentic assessment' or 'assessment for learning' (see Black et al. 2003; Klenowski 2011; Lingard, Mills & Hayes 2006; Newmann & Associates 1996; Swaffield 2011; Torrance 1995). It is argued that having different assessment tasks that take into account student diversity, as long as the tasks are designed to work with the same learning objectives and assessment criteria and are intellectually challenging and meaningful, is an important means of ensuring that teachers are able to 'eliminate barriers to demonstrating achievement' (Tomlinson 2005, p.265).

In considering the relationship between assessment and differentiation there are also questions about the purposes of assessment. Regularly assessment is seen as the endpoint of a unit of work that assesses and ranks student performance. It is also sometimes seen as providing feedback to students on what their strengths are and where they need to improve. However, as much of the assessment literature cited above indicates, assessment is much more than that. It also provides important 'data' to teachers on what students know when beginning a unit of work, on what certain students need to focus on in terms of meeting the task expectations, what strategies the teacher is employing that are working and what needs changing, how these might differ for different students and what the teacher might need to do before undertaking this particular unit of work in the future. Such data would seem to be critical to a differentiated classroom that is concerned with ensuring that *all* students are able to meet the same criteria even if the products they create are delivered through a variety of media (McTighe & Brown 2005, p.239). However, as Moon (2005, p.228) has noted: 'assessment data gathered . . . are only helpful in improving instruction when teachers are willing to modify their practices based on the data'. Such modifications are also only likely when the assessment focus is on more than just the grades that students receive for particular pieces of work.

Pedagogical differentiation at Red Point High

Differentiation had been an issue for both schools in this study. Indeed their mediocre audit outcomes on differentiation, and their desire to improve the practice across the school, had been a key motivation for their engagement with this research. However, in this chapter we focus on Red Point High. Red Point High makes an interesting case study as the principal at the school was a strong advocate for differentiation; he had strong views about what it might look like in the classroom and he had been a member of one of the audit teams evaluating Queensland government schools. As such he wanted to ensure that differentiation was widespread across Red Point High. Thus, as part of the research design we were allocated a small group of teachers to work with to develop their understandings of differentiation. We began by interviewing approximately 20 school personnel, and over the course of the project most were interviewed on more than one occasion. Next we began work with a small group of approximately 10 teachers to trial different approaches to differentiation; they then shared their various experiences in workshops we facilitated. The teachers were mostly female and ranged in age and teaching experience.

At Red Point High, as with Crimson High, the school had invested heavily in analysing their quantitative data, establishing dedicated positions within their schools to interpret the data and provide a framework for identifying students 'at risk' by placing students in different 'bands'. This approach filtered through to our initial discussions with teachers who often adopted the same lens through which to construct concepts of diversity within their classrooms:

> In Year 9 Geography [I have a] very diverse range of students in that class. I'm doing an analysis of that class's results in Term 1. There's a mix of students in Band 4 all the way through to Band 9, so that's a very diverse class. (Jen)

The use of the term 'diverse' in this particular extract illustrates the increasing tendency to associate understandings of diversity with the grouping of students according to their academic results. This emphasis on quantitative data-gathering to understand students' experiences of schooling can produce two effects; first it can displace the varied and nuanced ways that teachers come to know their students, the knowledge and skills that students bring to the classroom and the fluctuating environment in which learning occurs; second, it can privilege quantitative over qualitative data and depersonalise the ways teachers think about students (a binary construct that labels students as either academically successful or 'at risk'), undervaluing the complex relationship between teacher and student and the process of teaching and learning. Many of the teachers in our study indicated that a focus on quantitative results alone worked to untether the process of teaching and learning from the daily interactions between students and teachers. In privileging quantitative data-gathering about students, the words of Polesel et al. (2012) have a lot of purchase: 'shift[ing] from a focus on the needs of the child (and the associated responsiveness to the child's needs) to a focus on the needs of the system' (p.11).

This quantitative framing of diversity according to 'bands' shaped many of our initial discussions with teachers. Conscious of the current policy context and the pressures on schools and teachers, teachers felt there was an underlying expectation from the school's senior administrators that they would need to link any intervention strategies developed during the research project to their implementation of 'Curriculum into the Classroom'.[2] This 'curriculum package' contained detailed planning documents specifying what students needed to learn in whole school curriculum and assessment plans, year level plans, unit plans, lesson overviews, assessment instruments and assessment marking guides. As with differentiation, there was some confusion amongst the teachers in this school (as well as across the State) about the status of these materials. The introduction of the materials into the Queensland government system was highly controversial, with some teachers feeling it was an attempt to 'teacher proof' the new Australian Curriculum, some with the view that it was highly restrictive and some that its expectations of students were far too high. In many ways these concerns about expectations were linked to the teaching timeline that teachers felt was too demanding:

> The objectives in the actual Australian curriculum . . . there's things where the time constraints they put into the C2C aren't realistic.
>
> (Aisha)

> I feel in Science, the C2C [doesn't] allow for deep understanding. . . . You might have one or two lessons to gloss over it, 'Did you get that kids? We've got to go on'.
>
> (Bianca)

Our workshops with teachers often began with an airing of the frustrations they felt in relation to the constant pressure of trying to teach and assess curriculum content in a short amount of time. As one teacher indicated:

> It has just been an absolute nightmare and you have to cover it [curriculum content] because for the test, you have to somehow get [the students] there and their marks are down and because they haven't done the previous units in Year Eight and Nine . . . the Grade Tens are suffering unbelievably . . . they're just so far behind it's ridiculous.
>
> (Cherie)

In such a pressured environment teachers felt they had little time to understand the needs of their individual students within the confines of the larger group needs; rather, there was a push to ensure that the class as a whole completed the curriculum units within the allocated time. Much of the early workshop discussions therefore were based on teachers' beliefs that if they had more time to 'teach', rather than 'cram and test', they would be able to develop a range of effective strategies that better suited the needs of their students. Differentiation therefore was necessarily linked to having time in an otherwise crowded curriculum.

Understandings of differentiation

One of the main features of Red Point High's interpretation of differentiation had been to equate it with streaming classes or setting up mixed ability groups within classes. It was suggested that the school's approach to streaming under the previous principal had been instrumental in its good outcomes and that differentiation was supportive of this approach. Red Point High has not been alone in considering 'ability grouping' as a means of lifting academic standards (Ireson & Hallam 1999); nor indeed in seeing differentiation as another term for streaming. For example, Terwell (2005, p.653), in his work on curriculum differentiation writes, 'curriculum differentiation, i.e. streaming, tracking, ability-grouping, is one of the most persistent issues in curriculum theory and practice'. Interestingly this view tended to be held by teachers rather than the principal. Indeed the principal was highly critical of this association, arguing that whilst many within the school thought that they were doing differentiation well, this was not the case. Phil stated:

> And I think probably for too long people here have felt we're differentiating because we've got basically streamed classes. That's not differentiation.

His view was that differentiation involved diverse ability, or heterogeneous, classes where the teacher set activities to meet the needs of all the students in the class. He told us:

> Differentiation is 'in my class of 25 . . . I've got 25 different kids with different abilities and making sure I've got learning tasks happening that are appropriate to their needs'. It's hard work–no doubt it's the hardest aspect of teaching, I think.

He went on to explain what this might look like in the classroom. He described a hypothetical class to us where differentiation would be occurring. In this class of 25 students he envisaged the 'high flyers' undertaking independent work, whilst the teacher was working with other groups of students who were struggling, and a teacher's aide was in the classroom supporting individuals or very small groups who had trouble with their reading. He stressed that these groups would not be fixed, but 'fluid': 'It shouldn't be locked in to, you know, this person is always going to be in that middle group, or the lower group'. He suggested that there were not many teachers in the school who were interpreting differentiation in this way.

While Phil had a clear image of effective differentiation, our focus teachers felt uncertain about what was expected of them. One teacher in particular, Lucy, highlighted the way in which she struggled with what was expected of her. She told us how as part of her trial and error approach to implementing differentiation she had tried three different types of groups. In the first instance, she organised the class into groups on the basis of current achievement levels. She explained that this meant that:

> I was almost writing for five different classes every time I had a lesson with those kids. . . . I tried that for a week–and I ended up spending the majority of my time with my low level kids, because they need so much structure and assistance and help to get through even minimal tasks. And I almost felt guilty because I was neglecting my high-end kids, because they are capable of doing things on their own. But when Sandra said to me on the way out 'I felt like I haven't seen you for a week, Miss', I thought right, it's got to go, it's not working that way. . . .

This had a big impact upon Lucy because, as she told us, Sandra was 'probably my top kid'. She noted that it had not been a conscious decision to leave the high achiever groups on their own, 'but that's how it happened, just because the other kids were more needy'. She went on to outline how as a consequence of not being able to support many of the students in the class because of the amount of time she was spending with the students who needed the greatest support, she set up mixed ability groups.

> So then I tried mixed ability groups. . . . I felt like that failed as well, because the (lower level) kids relied really heavily on who the (level) B kids were.

Lucy had hoped that the 'peer coaching' that could take place within this structure would be a great benefit to both the high and lower achieving students in the groups. However, she suggested that the different motivation levels and the willingness of the lower achieving students to defer to those obtaining better grades than them meant that the quality of learning was affected. As a consequence she claimed:

> I felt like they learnt nothing in that week, that I tried mixed ability. Because they were just either copying–or agreeing, or being apathetic about the decisions that were being made.

The third form of grouping that she tried was based on friendships. She indicated that: 'That was probably the most successful grouping that I had for that class'. She suggested that within friendship groups the students had close relationships with each other and strong commitments to making sure that the group dynamics worked. She explained that this might have been because she set tasks that had to be completed before students were allowed to leave to go out to recess. Thus when asked why she thought it had been so successful she replied: 'Only because I think they generally care about each other enough to want to help each other to get out the classroom at the time–that's the motivation'. However, there did also appear to be other factors. She talked about how she also changed her classroom activities a lot with the new friendship groups in order to make the class work more engaging:

> . . . it wasn't a concrete sheet that had to be done, or a concrete activity, or a table that had to be filled out–like, there had to be genuine discussion and that had to be–they had to decide, and make opinions, and make judgments. . . . And I knew that I could do conversationy type stuff with those groups, because they're already used to conversing and they already respect each other. But if I tried to do that in, say–I don't know–mixed ability groups, I can't see that they would value each other's opinions. . . .

She also indicated that the first two forms of grouping were resented by the students who did not want to be told which groups that they had to belong to. This aligns with those arguments by Tomlinson and others that a lack of student voice, or representation (Fraser 2009), in the classroom has an impact upon their motivation and engagement in class.

In contrast to the grouping of students, Florence interpreted differentiation as a need to construct individual learning plans for every student. In high school, this could entail the preparation of up to 150 different plans! The situation of individualised learning plans came up at one of our group meetings, where Florence–who had been extremely enthusiastic about differentiated learning–suggested to our focus group of teachers that they should have individualised work plans and that she had a plan for every one of her students. She told us during a group discussion why she was prepared to do this:

> Because I feel very strongly about all my kids having opportunities to succeed in everything and so I just feel very happy about it. I do spend a lot of hours working but, that is my goal to have individualised learning plans for all of my students and . . . I do think it is possible.

Many of the other teachers appeared incredulous at this claim, and indeed due to her perceived expertise on differentiation became highly critical of such expectations. The principal, Phil, seemed to share these teachers' views about the un-tenability of such an approach to differentiation:

> It's a tough ask to say there's 25 different kids in the class–everyone gets an individualised program. . . . I mean that's just bizarre. Like, you know, the workload would be ridiculous.

In addition to grouping and individualised plans, teachers were confused or at odds about other key aspects of differentiation. Assessment in relation to differentiation, for example, was also raised as a contentious issue. For some teachers differentiation meant trying to construct different assessment tasks to ensure that students could achieve success and had the opportunity to demonstrate their strengths rather than their weaknesses. Some teachers were upset that they had been told that they were not allowed to change assessment tasks for different groups of students. Lucy, who had been enthusiastic in her engagement with differentiation, and whose efforts to differentiate through class groupings were outlined above, told us:

> I think that's the key ingredient–being able to change the assessment piece, so that every single kid is able to–you're able to better reach every single kid. Like I've got kids in my low level grade 10 class that can't write an essay, but they'd do an amazing play script if I was able to. . . . I think there's always going to be some reason, and some situations, where kids have to learn to write an essay – . . . but being able to change some of the assessment pieces, some of the time, would be really, really handy. . . .

Another teacher commented:

> I'd love nothing more than to have levels in my assessments constantly so that every time, every assessment it was differentiated so that kids could pick

> even the mode of delivery. . . . I'd like to differentiate every assessment to have at least three levels for my Grade Ten class, but, we're not allowed to in English. . . .
>
> (Mary)

This policy appeared to vary across the different curriculum areas. Within the mathematics subject areas in the non-senior years, teachers suggested that the assessment tasks catered to different levels. However, this appeared to relate to such practices as extension tests for the high achieving mathematics students. In the main the policy in each department in the school appeared to be that there was a common assessment system in which all students participated.

There was also some discussion about the extra support students were entitled to in order to complete assessment tasks, especially exams. Lucy expressed concern that such support was limited to those students who had been ascertained or who were deemed to be an English as a Second Language (ESL) student. She stated: 'I just hate that kids only get extra support if they've been officially labelled with something'. During the same discussion, another teacher went on to raise concerns about her students whom she knew would struggle with the demands of exams:

> You see them sitting in exams because we have to go and supervise them and there are so many kids that are in our literacy, numeracy classes that we know would benefit just by someone [a support teacher] being there in the exam room and they're not allowed to and every year we ask if we could please have these kids come and sit in a supervised class with us and they say 'no' every single time.
>
> (Sonia)

For some of these teachers, a failure on the part of some departments to differentiate through extra support for those students who were clearly struggling at school was seen as an equity issue that was not being addressed at the school.

What is evident from these short excerpts is that some teachers, like Lucy, are clearly grappling with differentiation in the classroom. Whilst others, like Florence, have very firm ideas about what constitutes differentiation, that view is not shared by other teachers, or indeed by the principal, who by having been selected to be an auditor was deemed to be an expert on differentiation. There were even tensions across departments with very different responses to issues such as differentiating assessment tasks. The uncertainty surrounding the meaning of differentiation would seem to highlight the difficulty schools faced in obtaining an 'outstanding' on this aspect of the Teaching and Learning Audit.

Competing demands

At the time of our work with the teachers at Red Point High the Australian government was in the process of introducing a new national curriculum, the Australian Curriculum, in the areas of science, mathematics and English, with history, and then other curriculum areas to follow soon after. In order to facilitate the implementation of this curriculum, the Queensland Department of Education developed a set of resources referred to as C2C (Curriculum into the Classroom) (Department of Education and Training 2016). When the materials were first launched the then Director General of Education was reported as saying that all government schools and teachers had to follow C2C curriculum documents, lesson by lesson. However, this was moderated within weeks to suggest that only those schools that had not excelled on the Teaching and Learning Audits were expected to implement C2C verbatim, and then soon after that, the call was that each school had flexibility in how they were used. The final official line was that the materials could be adapted and that they were not compulsory. For instance, a factsheet distributed by the Department of Education and Training (2016, p.1) stated: 'the C2C materials provide a starting point for curriculum planning–it is not mandatory for schools to use them'. However, within Red Point High the message, according to the teachers, was that they were to be implemented as written. This caused much anguish on the part of the teachers in our research group (see Gowlett et al. 2014).

In particular, teachers were concerned that the restrictive nature of the C2C materials and the time constraints imposed on them by the demands of the C2C materials meant that implementing differentiation would be even more difficult than it would be in other contexts. There was also a sense that the materials did not allow sufficient time to be concentrated on any one topic; as previously mentioned, teachers felt that time constraints were not realistic, and that these prevented the students from gaining a deep understanding of complex matters.

Some teachers also felt there was an underlying expectation from the school's senior administrators that they would need to link their work with differentiation into the implementation of the C2C materials. Indeed, the C2C lessons plans had, according to teachers, 'one little column' for indicating how they had differentiated in each lesson. One of the workshops with teachers began with an airing of the frustrations they felt in relation to the constant pressure of trying to teach and assess curriculum content in a short amount of time. For the teachers it was a nightmare, and the students' marks were down. As well, many students were a long way behind on some subjects. In such a pressured environment teachers felt they had little time to understand the needs of their individual students within the confines of the larger group needs; rather, there was a push to ensure that the class as a whole completed the curriculum units within the allocated time.

Recognition of difference and C2C

In some cases the demands were seen to work against building students' interests and cultures into the curriculum. For instance, one mathematics teacher (Dianne) told us:

> There's also no time to teach things properly and I mean, looking at quadratics, there's so many applications. You could talk about Angry Birds, the path of the Angry Bird and their favourite game these days, that's a parabola,

> that's what this is all about and that would be perfect, but you might only have time to talk about it for five minutes and then all you've got to do is hope that they can do the equations in their books, in their books and that's it. They've crammed it in so much you can't explore anything cool about maths anymore and it's just, the kids are just hating maths.

This cramming, for which C2C was blamed, was seen as being counter-productive to developing students' 'deep understanding'. Some teachers suggested that this was in part due to the materials being focussed on the needs of the 'middle students' through an approach that valorised 'chalk and talk' and 'rote learning'. Within the teachers' complaints were echoes of Ted Sizer's (1992) famous notion of 'less is more', as Jen stated:

> See, I think it was better when I had to cover half the curriculum that you do now for those lower level kids, but the thing is, they probably learnt, apart from the difficult questions, they probably learnt 80 per cent of that and can retain that whereas now you're doing double the amount of work and retaining very, very little. I can't get them to retain very much at all.

For some of the teachers the C2C materials worked against the needs of those students who struggled with the expectations of schooling. There were those who suggested that along with denying teachers the professional space to accommodate student interests, the materials were also pitched at too high a level without appropriate scaffolding. The following comment by Aisha captured the sentiment of many other teachers:

> I'm finding the results of my kids are suffering. Last year I had quite a lot of success with some low level literacy classes because I was able to teach content that directly appealed to them, but that choice was taken out of our hands now and for better or for worse, that's what's happened, so I'm finding that the kids aren't as engaged or nearly even close to caring as much as what they did and it's quite frustrating for everybody involved and even my high flyers, it's hard, it's hard.

Whilst many of the teachers complained that the C2C materials were far too complex for many of the students in their classes, and that the lack of flexibility worked against them having an opportunity to develop activities that would engage the students, there were also concerns expressed, as above, about the 'high flyers'. For example, Bianca argued that the materials did not extend her students:

> Maybe English is different, but I found that it really is targeted towards the lower end of the stream, especially in Grade Ten and I'm finding that it's my high flyers that are missing out and that I'm not able to differentiate like extending them anymore because they're just stuck in a rut of doing the same boring stuff as everybody else and there's not a chance to help extend

them anymore because you're too busy trying to catch everybody else up to where they've got to be. It really is aimed at the lower mid kid. I only teach Grade Ten English, I don't teach Eights and Nines.

'Knowing' students and differentiation

A key component of a successfully differentiated classroom would appear to be based on the teachers' knowledge of their students. The teachers indicated that the way in which they had to power through the materials in order to keep up with expectations meant that the slowness of pace needed to develop such knowledge was not possible. Cherie stated:

> I feel more than ever, high school at least if not all of education at the moment is a sausage grinder. We're just making sausages and we don't care about the quality of the sausages. There's no chance to re-teach things, there's no chance to slow down, fill in the gaps. There's nothing.

The apparent mandated nature of the materials and lack of support for professional judgement and decision-making was also seen as an inhibitor for knowing and understanding the students. As Bianca noted:

> So for English, because we, we used to be able to choose your topics that you taught, the novels that you picked on, we had two weeks or three weeks in class with the learners and go 'OK, this book's going to suit them because a lot of them are interested in this idea' and then teach your unit based on that, so you all had to do an analytical essay, but you could choose the novel, ways that you go about it, the content, the way you taught it, but it's just like 'it's Australian', so it's like 'the theme is Australia, this is how you go about it'. You can't even choose your theme or ways that you want to approach it.

Many of the teachers were beginning to feel the contradictory pressures of trying to implement mandated curriculum and pedagogical practices that did not align with what they saw as effective approaches to the teaching of their students in quite emotional ways. For example, Aisha stated:

> Oh you struggle not to cry yourself to sleep sometimes. It makes you feel, 'like what's the point of being a teacher if we can't actually teach them'.

Other teachers concurred with this sentiment.

Indigenous perspectives and C2C

As many of the group meetings had involved discussions about social justice, and in particular Nancy Fraser's understandings of social justice, the conversation raised issues about the ways in which the valuing of difference could be enhanced through approaches to differentiation, and the way in which the C2C materials impacted upon this. The main area of concern related to Indigenous education (see Chapter 6 for further discussion of Indigenous education). For many of the teachers, there was a feeling that the materials only engaged with Indigenous issues in a tokenistic and stereotypic way. For example, Cherie told us:

> It makes me laugh all the time, the C2C units, they always have a bit there about introducing Indigenous perspectives, so they'll throw in the yarning circle. Let's sit around and do it in the yarning circle and that's it, you tick that box. So the yarning circle comes up an awful lot. . . . There are units that are focusing on Indigenous perspectives as well, but generally it seems like every so often you'll come across and there'll just be, thrown in this token of a yarning circle.

When asked how they could avoid such a tokenistic approach, most teachers had their own ideas. In some cases these ideas might have been challenged in relation to their appropriateness, for example, as with the term 'legends' used below. However, as with this case, there was an intent to utilise Indigenous knowledges as part of the everyday curriculum:

> Well there's some genuine ones like in Science the other day, we were talking about the three sisters and the Aboriginal legend that goes with that and I've been doing that for years, it's not because somebody said to me 'now you've got to start including it', but it's just that those legends are quite interesting to the kids on rock formations that the Indigenous population has had, so that was a genuine case because as I said, I've been doing it because the kids have enjoyed it and I've been doing it for years from, that sort of thing.
>
> (Dianne)

Another teacher stated:

> It really depends on your teaching area because drama, I can use it a lot. Our Year Nines, we do rituals and that's a good avenue for me to be able to introduce, we do storytelling and that type of thing and talk about how rituals started and what they were used for and what they're all about and their assessment unit at the end, they get to choose based on their interest what ritual they wanted to do, so they could do a modern one like a wedding type ceremony or they could look at doing something more of the dreamtime, so I suppose depending on your subject area, it allows for you to be able to make it a part of it rather than just a token.
>
> (Mary)

When asked about how they incorporated the interests of Indigenous students into their classes, they indicated how they took group differences into account:

> I think especially in drama, I find a lot of Indigenous students are really ashamed to hop up on stage. They're happy to have class attention if they're

> mucking around, but as soon as you put them on the stage they're embarrassed, so having that avenue to teach it, I ask them if they have any stories to tell and then they can get engaged in that and they tell their stories. I say 'how could you put that to some movement?' and that type of thing. I think by doing that, if I didn't have Indigenous students in the class, I don't think that activity would be as good as it is because the kids listen, they know what they're talking about and then they ask them lots of questions, 'what do you mean your Granddad . . . so what . . .' and I think it's good for both of them, but I don't think it would be as good an activity if I didn't have the Indigenous students.
>
> (Lucy)

These data add to the argument made earlier that differentiation needs more theoretical and practical definition and teachers need more support to explore this in their work. Considering, for example, the comments above, we can see many problematics in how Indigeneity is constructed and connectedness is defined. While the interests of the Indigenous students are recognised here, there are obvious tensions evident such as an essentialising of Indigenous learner identities and assumptions of knowing and being based on these identities. We explore these issues later in this book.

An interesting side story to our study is that had the school not performed poorly in their eyes on the Teaching and Learning Audit in relation to differentiation, we might not have been given the opportunity to work with these teachers, which in turn provided them with space to trial various approaches to differentiation in their attempts to understand its purposes and practicalities. We recognise that not every teacher is in the position of those at Red Point High in that they can be provided with space to work closely with academics to engage in professional dialogue about a particular reform. However, we would stress that it is these very conversations that are critical to pedagogical reforms that can benefit students.

Differentiation and social justice

The audit culture and top-down management of curriculum reform created high levels of anxiety for many teachers as they attempted to make sense of the multiple ways in which they were being assessed and judged. This was the case at Red Point High.

The way in which teachers at Red Point High took up the mandate of differentiated learning, as prescribed in the Queensland Teaching and Learning Audit, offers a number of lessons about both differentiation and pedagogical reform and their impact upon teachers. There were clearly different understandings and mobilisations of differentiation amongst teachers, by the school administration and across different faculties in the school. These different understandings were shaped and informed by the audit culture operating in Queensland government schools. To some extent this culture has inhibited socially just practices in schools, as narrow forms of differentiation based around streaming and setting have been maintained. There is also a way in which the increased surveillance of teachers can work towards them taking 'safe' options rather than attempting significant reforms. However, some of the teachers' stories at Red Point High indicate that our collaborative work on differentiation freed them somewhat from top-down policy approaches that come with punitive/surveillance measures, and opened possibilities for a richer engagement with the underpinning rationale for those policies to occur. Through these discussions it became apparent that differentiation can align nicely with a social justice agenda in schools. For instance, it is concerned with ensuring that all children are challenged intellectually in the classroom, that teachers take into account student background to ensure that the learning is meaningful, that active learning is encouraged, that spaces are created for student voices to be heard and that student differences are respected and taken into account. However, one cause for concern is the way in which the policy mandate for differentiation is legitimising the streaming of classes, as was the case in some sections of the case study school. The inequities generated by such practices have long been identified (see for example, Ireson & Hallam 1999), and indeed many advocates of pedagogical differentiation are often highly opposed to streaming (see George 2005). Unfortunately, as Boaler argued back in 1997 (p.165), greater competition between schools, marketisation and league tables has 'meant that setting is now back in vogue and schools are returning to policies of differentiation and polarisation . . . in alarming numbers'. It is quite possible that pressures around such policies as the Teaching and Learning Audit will ensure that such streaming and setting practices are still seen as the appropriate way to differentiate (see Chapter 3).

The individualised approach to differentiation, sometimes seen as a counterpoint to streaming, raised by one of the teachers at the school, is also questionable as an effective and appropriate response to differentiating a classroom. Individualised programs for high school students are problematic on at least two levels. First, as recognised by the principal, it is a workload issue for teachers. Whilst we would suggest that it is important for teachers to know their students and to try and understand the ways in which they can be stimulated and motivated to learn, an individual program for every student when a teacher might have up to six different classes is almost impossible to create. Secondly, and perhaps a more serious concern, is the way in which problems with learning can be individualised. Increasingly disadvantage is seen as an individual problem rather than as a problem created through systemic or structurally driven inequities and injustices. With such a view of the world, oppressions brought about through, for example, differences in gender, race, ethnicity, class, sexuality and age are often washed out of pedagogical considerations. When this occurs, group identity, or indeed solidarity, is not encouraged. We would suggest, as indeed much of the pedagogical differentiation literature does (see Jackson 2005; de Jager 2013), that students from marginalised backgrounds will benefit from having their cultures valued in the classroom, and that those from more privileged backgrounds will also reap the benefits from pedagogical practices that expose them to rich and diverse forms of knowledge and understandings about the world.

We are also concerned, as were some of the teachers in our study, that differentiation might lead to a watered down curriculum and low expectations of students, especially if assessment tasks offered differing levels of intellectual challenge. We are of the view that differentiating learning *and* assessment in a classroom can still be challenging and meaningful (de Jager 2013). Here we think of the assessment literature that suggests that students be provided with real world problems that are related to student interests (see Hayes et al. 2006). As we have indicated earlier, differentiation can be about removing the barriers to demonstrating what students have learnt; we would suggest that what should be of concern to educators is finding ways for students to showcase their learning. This might mean that some students are given extra time, extra resources and support, have input into the construction of tasks, and have a range of choice about how to present their knowledge, skills and understandings. However, the expectations around quality should not be different.

The shift by some teachers to a survival mode of pedagogy (teach more content in less time) following the introduction of the Australian Curriculum and C2C required students to keep up or fail. This increased pressure on students to learn curriculum content outside of allocated class time and pressured their parents to provide more support outside of school. Ironically, the survival mode of pedagogy was instigated by higher expectations of what students could and should know, but this actually forced teachers to skim the surface of topics and rely more on the capacity of students to learn beyond the classroom. From a social justice perspective such pedagogical regimes within and beyond school will reproduce existing inequalities because students with knowledgeable and resource rich parents will be able to keep up through tutoring support and direct assistance on assignments. Differentiation in such contexts follows existing lines of privilege rather than challenging them. Time to teach remains at the heart of a differentiated pedagogy, so a key policy challenge is to balance the demands in the prescribed curriculum with the provision of sufficient pedagogical time. Failure to address this balance will reproduce established inequalities and work against social justice outcomes from schooling.

One positive contribution of the audit had been that the school had begun discussions around pedagogy. This was apparent in the staff meetings and in the conversations after visits to teachers' classrooms by the school leadership team. However, much of this had the tone of surveillance. We, as was the case with many of the participating teachers in our study, are not opposed to accountability in teachers' work with their students. However, there is a sufficient amount of literature to suggest that narrow forms of accountability can lead to teachers (and schools) 'fabricating' an image that best meets what are perceived to be the requirements of prevailing discourses (see Ball 2003; Keddie, Mills & Pendergast 2011). In the case of differentiation, where there is a lack of knowledge about what it entails and where there is pressure from an external audit and classroom visits from a leadership team (some of whom were identified by teachers as also not having a good understanding of differentiation), the responses appeared to lack substance. Indeed in our many observations of classes we were struck by the lack of active learning, by a lack of engagement with difference and young people's backgrounds and cultures and indeed the lack of intellectual quality. However, we also came across many thoughtful teachers who cared about their students, and who put a lot of effort in to the preparation and delivery of their classes. It very much appeared that this lack of pedagogical differentiation was not due to any deficit in the teachers, but in the failure of the system to create the appropriate environment for them to enact and trial the forms of pedagogy that align with differentiation. Hence, a 'perverse effect' (Lingard & Sellar 2013) of Queensland's Teaching and Learning Audit may be that many teachers did not have time to develop deep understandings of what it would mean to differentiate their classrooms and fell back on what they knew best, streaming, setting, individualised plans and different quality tasks.

It was also clear that one of the 'perverse effects' of the Teaching and Learning Audit was the creation of uncertainty about what was expected of teachers. This was made especially the case with very little professional support around differentiation in the lead up to the audit. However, it appears from the work done at Red Point High that it is possible to work in the spaces created by the audit in order to pursue a social justice agenda. That said, as is apparent here, differentiation is a complex concept, not easy to shift from policy to classroom context, and perhaps requires more careful explication at the policy level and also more support for teachers to enact. We would also suggest that in order for worthwhile innovations to reach classrooms through policy, teachers need to be convinced of their merit. Teachers are unlikely to acquire this conviction when simply compelled to implement reforms; particularly if policy reform does not acknowledge the time and space needed at the classroom level for teachers to understand their students' specific characteristics, strengths, needs and experiences. Understanding these things can help teachers define a social justice agenda that can be interpreted meaningfully for their specific context. As teachers in our case study demonstrated, when given the space to experiment with a particular pedagogical strategy, in this case differentiation, many teachers are very willing to work in productive–learner responsive–ways to see how they might best meet the needs of their students.

As a consequence of this concern with what was happening in the classrooms, the seventeen-person leadership team at the school (heads of department, deputy principals and the principal) were each allocated four classes to visit and observe. They were to collect data on a range of practices with a focus on student engagement. We were told 'that it will all get collated on a spreadsheet to get a sort of snapshot of a week at Red Point'. What was apparent was that part of this information was being sought to ensure that the principal could meet his accountability expectations. For instance, he indicated that if he was asked if he knew whether or not the Australian Curriculum[3] was being implemented in his school, 'I could say "OK, it's been implemented", but "how do I know?"–"Because I've gone into classes"'. However, the class visits were not solely about ensuring that teachers were conforming to various mandates; they were also seen as having a role in creating professional dialogue as after each observation there was a meeting between the staff member and the leadership team member about what had been seen in the classroom.

Whilst the audit had led to this increased surveillance of teachers, it also led to changes in the organisation of staff meetings. It was reported that every second staff meeting was now devoted to professional dialogue and in-service on a number of educational topics, including behaviour management and using data. Discussion was seen as being critical to improving practice. It was at these staff meetings where differentiation had been discussed by the whole staff. At one of these meetings differences in understandings between various faculties had been foregrounded. For instance, we were told that it was apparent that there were people in the Arts Faculty who had been doing differentiation 'forever': 'They've got–like, in visual art–or in music–you know, they're basically designing their own art work, choosing what medium they want to use. There's so much capacity for individualised and personalised learning'. On the other hand, there were some faculties where there was significant resistance to differentiation; the mathematics department was highlighted as one of those.

The politics of instigating a major pedagogical reform at the same time as a new curriculum would on the face of it appear to make sense. As other research has indicated, pedagogy, curriculum and assessment are closely interconnected (Bernstein 1971; Hayes et al. 2006). However, the C2C framework in Queensland was not seen by many of the teachers we interviewed as being complementary. Instead, this reform was seen as an imposition that took them away from the business of teaching. Furthermore, the lesson plans that were contained within these materials were seen as being in conflict with the notion of differentiation. For example, they were seen to homogenise the student body; in some cases as operating at a low level, in other instances at too high a level. There were no teachers who indicated that the materials helped them to differentiate their classrooms. Instead they suggested that little attention was given to this. They even suggested that in relation to taking account of Indigenous issues in education, there was a trivialising of difference. We take up the issue of differentiation and support for Indigenous students in Chapter 6. However, it is important to stress here that for these teachers, the social justice spaces opened up by the focus on differentiation were under pressure from the compulsion to take up what were perceived as mandated curriculum materials.

Conclusion

In this chapter we have been concerned with the politics surrounding the mandate to implement differentiated pedagogy in one Queensland high school. There was clearly much confusion amongst these teachers as to what constitutes differentiation. They would not be alone in this. As we explored the concept with the teachers in the school and engaged in the literature with them, it was apparent that pedagogical differentiation could work to leverage concerns with social justice.

As many of the teachers recognised, issues of distribution to some extent determined who received a quality education. Whilst at times the language did resort to deficit constructions of some students, e.g. 'low achievers', there was a suggestion that the struggle some students faced at school was not due to faults of their own, but rather that the curriculum failed to meet their needs. The pressure to differentiate also facilitated discussions around difference and the importance of teachers understanding students' cultural backgrounds. Some of the teachers in the group raised concerns about lack of student voice. Although this was not an overwhelming issue for teachers, much of the differentiation literature recognises that teachers need to consult young people regarding matters related to their learning.

However, no matter how differentiation was conceived, many of its social justice possibilities were constrained by existing policy frameworks. For example, the audit culture based on surveillance inhibited teachers' freedom and willingness to make pedagogical decisions that differentiation requires. Furthermore, time constraints imposed by curriculum reforms being implemented at the same time as this focus on differentiation worked against a thorough exploration of what differentiation might mean for these teachers' classrooms. This was compounded by the sense that many teachers felt the homogenising impulses of the C2C materials associated with the new Australian Curriculum also worked against the implementation of differentiation within their school.

The lessons here indicate that the implementation of pedagogical differentiation into classrooms does not sit outside of the everyday politics of school reform and broader neo-liberal agendas. We would suggest that to take up 'differentiation' in meaningful ways, and ways that will benefit all students, including those for whom school learning is often not a positive experience, will require an understanding by school leaders and those working in the policy arena that simply mandating a reform will not work. There have to be supports, time, trust, intellectual discussion and a commitment to ensuring that key principles of social justice are always foregrounded.

In the next chapter we explore the role of teacher expectations in relation to differentiation. A discourse of 'high expectations' was embedded as policy and voiced often and positively by the teachers we interviewed at Red Point High. However, the meaning of high expectations was complex and contradictory, revealing the influence of neo-liberal discourses promulgated in reports such as the internationally influential McKinsey Report (Barber & Mourshed 2007) and, in Queensland, the Masters Report (2009). For some teachers high expectations represented a demand on students regarding their behaviour and compliance with school norms. It generated concern amongst certain teachers that the standards at Red Point High might be undermined if the enrolment policy were to be relaxed. Rather than being an invitation to provide the highest quality schooling to all students who might enrol at Red Point High, it became a discourse related to maintaining the reputation of the school itself and resisting attempts to broaden the diversity of students at the school. However, as we have shown in this chapter, within the contested discourses on high expectations at Red Point High, there were opportunities for productive dialogue about differentiation and social justice.

Notes

1 See Education Queensland's Factsheet for parents and carers: http://education.qld.gov.au/nationalpartnerships/pdf/fact-sheet-carers.pdf.

2 See http://education.qld.gov.au/c2c/index.html for more details. During the course of our research project it was unclear whether it was mandatory for teachers to follow C2C.

3 The Australian Curriculum is Australia's first national curriculum and is being phased into the States and Territories at different rates. In 2012 Queensland introduced the English, Mathematics and Science curricula; History was introduced in 2013.

References

Apple, M 2005, 'Education, markets and an audit culture', *Critical Quarterly*, Vol. 47, nos. 1–2, pp.11–29.

Ball, S 2003, 'The teacher's soul and the terrors of performativity', *Journal of Education Policy*, Vol. 18, no. 2, pp. 215–228.

Ball, S 2012, *Global education Inc.: New policy networks and the neo-liberal imaginary*, Routledge, London.

Barber, M & Mourshed, M 2007, *How the world's best performing school systems come out on top*, McKinsey & Company, New York.

Bernstein, B 1971, 'On the classification and framing of educational knowledge', In *Knowledge and control: New directions for the sociology of education*, ed MFD Young, Collier-Macmillan, London, pp. 47–69.

Black, P, Harrison, C, Lee, C, Marshall, B, & William, D 2003, *Assessment for learning: Putting it into practice*, Open University Press, Maidenhead, UK.

Boaler, J 1997, 'When even the winners are losers: Evaluating the experiences of top set students', *Journal of Curriculum Studies*, Vol. 29, no. 2, pp. 165–182.

Coldron, J, Cripps, C, & Shipton, L 2010, 'Why are English secondary schools socially segregated?', *Journal of Education Policy*, Vol. 25, no. 1, pp. 19–35.

de Jager, T, 2013, 'Guidelines to assist the implementation of differentiated learning activities in South African secondary schools', *International Journal of Inclusive Education*, Vol. 17, no. 1, pp. 80–94.

Department of Education and Training (Qld) n.d. Teaching and learning audit: Smarter Schools National Partnerships fact sheet. http://education.qld.gov.au/nationalpartnerships/pdf/teaching-learning-audit.pdf. [17 November 2015].

Department of Education and Training 2016. Curriculum into the Classroom (C2C), http://education.qld.gov.au/c2c/. Accessed 2/8/2016.

Dixie, G 2011 'Differentiation: Setting learning objectives and outcomes', *Times Education Supplement*, 4 May. Available from: http://newteachers.tes.co.uk/content. [28 February 2014].

Everest, C 2003, 'Differentiation, the new monster in education: Differentiation is just another pressure meted out by managers', *The Guardian*, 18 February. Available from: https://www.theguardian.com/education/2003/feb/18/further education.uk4. [23 February 2015].

Fraser, N 1997, *Justice interruptus: Critical reflections on the 'postsocialist' condition*, Routledge, New York.

Fraser, N 2009, *Scales of justice: Reimagining political space in a globalizing world*, Columbia University Press, New York.

George, P 2005, 'A rationale for differentiating instruction in the regular classroom', *Theory Into Practice*, Vol. 44, no. 3, pp. 185–193.

Ginsberg, M 2005, 'Cultural diversity, motivation, and differentiation', *Theory Into Practice*, Vol. 44, pp. 218–225.

Gonzalez, L, Moll, N, & Amanti, C (eds) 2005, *Funds of knowledge: Theorizing practices in households, communities, and classrooms*, Lawrence Erlbaum, New Jersey.

Grek, S, Lawn, M, Lingard, B, & Varjo, J 2009, 'North by northwest: Quality assurance and evaluation processes in European education', *Journal of Education Policy*, Vol. 24, no. 2, pp. 121–133.

Hayes, D, Mills, M, Christie, P, & Lingard, B 2006, *Teachers and schooling Making a difference: Productive pedagogies, assessment and performance*, Allen & Unwin, Sydney.

Ireson, J & Hallam, S 1999, 'Raising standards: is ability grouping the answer?', *Oxford Review of Education*, Vol. 25, no. 3, pp. 343–358.

Jackson, Y 2005, 'Unlocking the potential of African American students: Keys to reversing underachievement', *Theory Into Practice*, Vol. 44, no. 3, pp. 203–210.

Keddie, A, Mills, M, & Pendergast, D 2011, 'Fabricating an identity in neo-liberal times: Performing schooling as "number one"', *Oxford Review of Education*, Vol. 37, no. 1, pp. 75–92.

Klenowski, V 2011, 'Assessment for learning in the accountability era: Queensland, Australia', *Studies in Educational Evaluation*, Vol. 37, no. 1, pp. 78–83.

Kronborg, L & Margaret Plunkett, M 2008, 'Curriculum differentiation: an innovative Australian secondary school program to extend academic talent', *The Australasian Journal of Gifted Education*, Vol. 17, no. 1, pp. 19–29.

Laitsch, D 2013, 'Smacked by the invisible hand: The wrong debate at the wrong time with the wrong people', *Journal of Curriculum Studies*, Vol. 45, no. 1, pp. 16–27.

Lingard, B Mills, M, & Hayes, D 2006, 'Enabling and aligning assessment for learning: Some research and policy lessons from Queensland', *International Studies in Sociology of Education*, Vol. 16, no. 2, pp. 83–103.

Lingard, B & Sellar, S 2013, '"Catalyst data": Perverse systemic effects of audit and accountability in Australian schooling', *Journal of Education Policy*, Vol. 28, no. 5, pp. 634–656.

Masters, G 2009, *A Shared Challenge: Improving literacy, numeracy and science learning in Queensland primary schools*. The Australian Council for Educational Research, Melbourne.

Masters, G 2010, *Teaching and learning: School improvement framework*, State of Queensland (Department of Education and Training) and the Australian Council for Educational Research *(ACER)*. Available from: http://research.acer.edu.au. [23 March 2014].

McTighe, J & Brown, J 2005, 'Differentiated instruction and educational standards: Is detente possible?', *Theory Into Practice*, Vol. 44, no. 3, pp. 234–244.

Moon, T 2005, 'The role of assessment in differentiation', *Theory Into Practice*, Vol. 44, no. 3, pp. 226–233.

Newmann, F & Associates 1996, *Authentic achievement: Restructuring schools for intellectual quality*, Jossey-Bass, San Francisco.

Noble, T 2004, 'Integrating the revised bloom's taxonomy with multiple intelligences: A planning tool for curriculum differentiation', *Teachers College Record*, Vol. 106, no. 1, pp. 193–211.

NSW Department of Education and Communities 2016, *Differentiating the curriculum*, State Government of New South Wales. Available from: http://www.curriculumsupport.education.nsw.gov.au. [23 February 2016].

OECD 2005, 'School factors related to quality and equity, results from PISA 2000', *State Government of Queensland*. Available from: http://education.qld.gov.au. [17 March 2014].

Polesel, J, Dulfer, N, & Turnbull, M 2012, 'The experience of education: The impacts of high stakes testing on school students and their families'. Literature Review prepared for the Whitlam Institute, Melbourne Graduate School of Education, and the Foundation for Young Australians. Available online at: http://www. whitlam. org/__data/assets/pdf_file/0008/276191/High_Stakes_Testing_Literature_ Review. pdf [20 September 2012].

Reynolds, D, & Teddlie, C 2002, *The international handbook of school effectiveness research*. Routledge, New York.

Sizer, T 1992, *Horace's School*, Houghton-Mifflin, Boston, MA.

Subban, P 2006, 'Differentiated instruction: A research basis', *International Education Journal*, Vol. 7, no. 7, pp. 935–947.

Swaffield, S 2011, 'Getting to the heart of authentic assessment for learning', *Assessment in Education: Principles, Policy & Practice*, Vol. 18, no. 4, pp. 433–449.

Terwel, J 2005, 'Curriculum differentiation: Multiple perspectives and developments in education', *Journal of Curriculum Studies*, Vol. 37, no. 6, pp. 653–670.

Tomlinson, CA 1995, 'Deciding to differentiate instruction in the middle school: One school's journey', *Gifted Child Quarterly*, Vol. 39, no. 2, pp. 77–114.

Tomlinson, CA 1999, 'Mapping a route toward differentiated instruction', *Educational Leadership*, Vol. 57, no. 1, pp. 12–16.

Tomlinson, CA 2000, 'Reconcilable differences', *Educational Leadership*, Vol. 58, no.1, pp. 6–11.

Tomlinson, CA 2005, 'Grading and differentiation: Paradox or good practice?', *Theory into Practice*, Vol. 44, no. 3, pp. 262–269.

Tomlinson, CA 2008, 'Goals of differentiation', *Educational Leadership*, Vol. 66, no. 3, pp. 26–30.

Torrance, H (ed) 1995, *Evaluating authentic assessment: problems and possibilities in new approaches to assessment*, Open University Press, Buckingham, UK.

Zipin, L, Sellar, S, & Hattam, R 2012, 'Countering and exceeding "capital": a "funds of knowledge" approach to re-imagining community', *Discourse: Studies in the Cultural Politics of Education*, Vol. 33, no. 2, pp. 179–192.

3 A politics of differentiation and teacher expectations

After the very first set of interviews at Red Point High we talked together as a research team about 'expectations' and how teachers at this school shared a common professional language centred on high expectations for their students and for the school. Comments by teachers included:

> We have high academic expectations for all children–which doesn't mean that all children will get As–all students in this school will be expected to improve the way they work; all students should believe that school will be value-adding.
>
> (Brian)

> (This school) stands out . . . in terms of high expectations of student behaviour, high expectations of academic performance.
>
> (Connie)

There was a sense of anticipation in the research team as we shared our impressions. We wondered how the teachers' discourses of high expectations at Red Point High might play out and whether their classroom practices could reveal some telling examples of socially just pedagogy. But we were also aware of the contemporary neo-liberal framing of high expectations that foregrounds rigorous standards for teachers and curricula, and supports policies of increased surveillance and accountability through national and international testing (Barber & Mourshed 2007; Masters 2009; Sahlberg 2011). We wondered how these competing discourses of social justice and neo-liberal performativity would play out with regard to teachers' expectations at Red Point High.

The issue of teachers' expectations was on our research radar prior to these first interviews at the school because we shared the assumption that any program of differentiation had to ensure high expectations for all students. As R.W. Connell noted in 1993, 'an education that privileges one child over another is giving the privileged child a corrupted education, even as it gives him or her a social or economic advantage. The issue of social justice is not an add-on. It is fundamental to what a good education is about' (Connell 1993, p.15). We wondered if a good education at Red Point High would bring together high expectations and a socially just approach to differentiation.

In this chapter we explore how the discourse of teacher expectations related to the politics of differentiation at Red Point High. As noted above, the term 'high expectations' was invoked often by the teachers we interviewed as a very positive aspect of the school's culture. However, we show in our analysis of the interviews that the meaning of high expectations was far from uniform. As mentioned in Chapter 2, the interviews revealed traces of the neo-liberal discourses promulgated in reports such as the McKinsey Report (Barber & Mourshed 2007) and in Queensland in the Masters Report (2009). To some teachers 'high expectations' made extra demands on students regarding their behaviour and compliance with school standards. Some teachers were concerned that the school's standards might be undermined if the enrolment policy was relaxed. Instead of being seen as a means of providing the highest quality schooling to all at Red Point High, high expectations became a means of maintaining the school's reputation and undermined attempts to broaden the diversity of students at the school. For other teachers, such as the Indigenous liaison worker, 'Aileen', and the welfare officer, 'Cassandra', 'high expectations' was an urgent call to address the needs of more marginalised students at the school. Likewise the principal, Phil, deployed high expectations as a critical lens to examine teaching in the lower-streamed classes and to challenge teachers to lift the quality of teaching offered to students most in need of support. As with the notion of differentiated pedagogy (see Chapter 2), high expectations could be deployed to close down options for productive dialogue or open up possibilities for dealing proactively with the more marginalised members of the school community. This chapter draws on the voices of Phil, Aileen and Cassandra as well as those of the deputy principal, 'Kath', and teachers 'Lenore', 'Nicola' and 'Helen' to explore these issues.

Social justice and teacher expectations

Nancy Fraser's (1997; 2009), framing of social justice in terms of redistribution, recognition and representation is particularly relevant in considering differentiation in relation to teacher expectations. Redistribution foregrounds consideration of how resource allocation is differentiated to ensure access for all students to the materials required for high quality education. Recognition points to the identity of students and how teachers' expectations are experienced by students as enabling or disabling. Representation directs attention to how opportunities are provided to students to be active agents within their own education and to participate in key decisions about their schooling. In the history of research on teacher expectations, the discriminatory effects of low teacher expectations on students from marginalised communities have been well documented. For example, James Rist's (1970) classic ethnographic study of urban classrooms revealed how the teachers' low expectations of children from a specific urban Black community dramatically influenced the poor quality of teaching provided, and the deplorable learning outcomes children were able to achieve across time. Rather than allowing ingrained and tacit low expectations to determine the quality of teaching provided to specific groups of students, a social justice agenda requires that teachers critically examine their expectations and find ways to engage all students in high quality learning activities. Following Rist's study (1970) and that of Rosenthal and Jacobson (1968) on the *Pygmalion effect*, social justice advocates for the last half century have challenged teachers to raise their expectations, to discard deficit thinking, to examine their political and social assumptions about marginalised groups in society and to reflect on their tacit and unexamined patterns of classroom interaction with students. The classroom interaction research of Brophy and Good (e.g. Brophy 1983; Brophy & Good 1972; Good 1987) and the micro-sociological research that followed Rist's study (e.g. Eder 1981; Mehan 1992) produced a wealth of evidence showing that children's opportunity to learn in the classroom is mediated by the differential expectations of teachers and the consequential patterns of interaction, learning tasks and assistance that teachers provide to children based on their expectations.

Research has shown that teachers' expectations are not idiosyncratic understandings of specific children but reflect common assumptions about the potential of children from different social and cultural groups (Ireson, Hallam & Hurley 2005). 'Potential' has become a popular term to describe appropriate expectations for different groups of students. A common repeated mantra is that 'every student should be able to reach his or her potential', but this mantra masks the influence of ingrained social and political discourses that lower judgements of potential for some groups in society. Typically, teachers expect more of children whose parents are employed in professional and white-collar jobs, whereas children from poor families, single-parent families or culturally marginalised communities are expected to struggle more at school. For example, Sorhagen (2013) investigated teacher expectations in 10 different national sites, and found that students from low-income backgrounds were most vulnerable to low teacher expectations. The general pattern of findings is that students from ethnic minorities and poorer families are highly likely to be assigned to lower streams and suffer the consequences of low expectations from their teachers. The knowledge and dispositions that these students bring to school are not valued or built upon by teachers and they become defined largely in terms of their deficits and deficiencies. Fraser's (1997; 2009) concept of recognition is relevant here. A social justice analysis of classrooms and schools requires teachers to recognise and value the funds of knowledge and cultural resources that students bring with them to schools (Comber 2016; Zipin 2009). This involves curriculum planning that incorporates the interests of children and it requires a pedagogy that deploys patterns of interaction and language formats that are familiar to children. In the context of Red Point High, Fraser's notion of recognition led us to interrogate the ways that teachers spoke about their expectations of different groups of students, particularly Indigenous students, and how admission to Red Point High was managed, particularly the criteria used for enrolment of students outside the normal catchment area for the school. The public management of the identity of the school as expecting high performance can function as a signal to the community of 'who is welcome here'.

Indigeneity and expectations

Discourse on high expectations among educators in Queensland, where Red Point High was situated, was also shaped at this time by the charismatic Indigenous educator, Chris Sarra (2005; 2014), who challenged teachers and the broader community to examine their expectations of Aboriginal and Torres Strait Islander students. His premise was that far too little is expected of Indigenous students and as a consequence the teaching that they receive is low quality and neglectful. He argued that deficit discourses amongst teachers posit that Indigenous children are less able to learn than their non-Indigenous counterparts because of their external situation (McNaughton & Mei Kuin Lai 2008; Sarra 2008). Such deficit discourses can be self-perpetuating, where preconscious patterns of assumption and thinking facilitate 'out of awareness searching for evidence to reinforce them' (Stronger Smarter Institute 2014, p.2). As principal of Cherbourg State School, Chris Sarra established a culture that directly challenged inherent deficit assumptions and low expectations (Sarra 2005). Teachers who were seen to be unprepared to lift their expectations of Indigenous students were 'invited' to leave the school, and he worked with students to enhance their self-perceptions by adopting a personal and collective motto of 'Strong and Smart'. He asked the students at the school to live up to this motto, and regularly visited classrooms where they celebrated their collective identity as Strong and Smart. As an Indigenous principal, Sarra also engaged with the parents and local Indigenous community to raise their expectations of what their children might achieve and who they might become. The success of his approach at Cherbourg, as revealed in improving attendance data and better learning outcomes, provided a platform for Sarra to establish the Stronger Smarter Institute with support from the Queensland State Government. We describe this recent history to highlight the prominence and potential of high expectations discourse for a social justice agenda, in particular with regard to marginalised students.

Streaming and expectations

We were also aware of the research literature on explicit and *de facto* streaming within schools. Research on streaming has demonstrated the negative effects that homogeneous achievement groups have on the most marginal groups in society (Sorhagen 2013). Streaming differentially benefits students placed in the top groups, whilst disadvantaging students placed in the low groups. Detailed statistical analyses conducted by Ireson, Hallam and Hurley (2005) indicated that streaming per se adds significantly to the variance in learning outcomes for students allocated to top versus bottom streams. These analyses controlled for factors such as prior achievement, gender and socio-economic status. This detailed research provides a convincing case that despite its apparent benefits in allowing more time for 'slower learners', and its workload attraction to teachers, streaming is not a socially just practice. Red Point High deployed streaming in the core curriculum areas of mathematics and English. It was puzzling to us, therefore, to hear teachers' passionate endorsement of high expectations for students whilst organising key curriculum areas to ensure that differential expectations were built into the structure of the school. As the deputy stated:

> We do have streaming in this school, but not to extremes, and with some mix. For example, we put kids with potential into classes where they get pushed. We try not to have classes of all Es. We try to mix gender too–I don't like same sex schools. A problem is that teachers tend to think 'these are Bs, Ds etc'–they make assumptions about kids.
>
> (Kath)

The appeal of streaming was perceived by teachers at Red Point High as simplifying their curriculum planning and making pedagogy more targeted and efficient. One teacher stated:

> Um, it (streaming) certainly does have its advantages in terms of, as a teacher you don't have to differentiate your learning or your teaching as much and you can then certainly spend the time with the kids who take a little bit longer. So, it has its benefits.
>
> (Lenore)

These efficiency goals of streaming were predicated on the assumption that students inherently have different potentials, but the research on steaming suggests it is the introduction of streaming per se that produces the differential levels of potential across time. Streaming practices concentrate specific groups of marginalised students into low streams and create powerful identity markers for such students about their capabilities and status at the school.

Initial reflections and puzzles

These various discourses on teachers' expectations entered our conversations as we conducted more interviews with teachers across the first weeks of data collection. Clear tensions and contradictions emerged between high expectations for all students but endorsement of streaming practices. It seemed that the school had designed a system of differentiation that would inevitably stigmatise certain students and groups as low achievers. There was also an ambiguity emerging for us regarding the actual focus of teachers on high expectations. Did teachers really mean high expectations for compliant behaviour from students rather than high expectations for deep learning across multifaceted curriculum areas? Also, we were now aware that discretionary admission to Red Point High from outside the catchment area was merit-based, and this concentrated high performing students in the school. As we noted in Chapter 1, there were some disgruntled long-term teachers who were unhappy about the recent increase in the number of Aboriginal and Torres Strait Islander students enrolled at the school. This suggested to us that the high expectations discourse for some teachers at Red Point High could actually be a discourse of exclusion. Rather than establishing a culture of inclusion for diverse groups of students, the high expectations discourse could be cover for a policy of creating an elite and homogenous school for the middle-class White community of the city.

So we completed the first period of data collection with a series of unresolved puzzles. We had identified discourses that related to our social justice framework, as well as a neo-liberal framing of expectations related to performativity and accountability. In addition, we began to hear an elitist discourse related to students' potential and an exclusionary discourse related to Indigeneity. It is necessary at this point to ask what discourses on 'teacher expectations' had been deployed in recent policy documents and pronouncements that had a direct influence on the work of teachers in schools across Queensland, including Red Point High.

Neo-liberal politics of high expectations

Teachers at Red Point High had a policy-driven imperative to reflect on their expectations, and consider whether their expectations were sufficiently 'high'. Schools across Queensland became enmeshed in a testing and accountability controversy following the publication in 2008 of the first NAPLAN results for literacy and numeracy. Teachers were positioned as personally accountable for their students' test results and they were castigated if they tried to 'excuse' (Masters 2009, p.85) poor results by appealing to contextual and out-of-school factors. Schools became preoccupied with managing their reputations as requiring high standards and expecting high performances from students. Later in this chapter we trace how *performativity* and *accountability* discourses were appropriated in the struggles within Red Point High regarding expectations for students.

The Masters Report (2009), entitled a *Shared Challenge*, was commissioned by an embattled State Government following the media release in late 2008 of the results of the first NAPLAN. The results were interpreted as a huge embarrassment for the State of Queensland and an indictment of the quality of teaching across the State. The Department of Education and Training (DET) summarised the results in the following terms:

> The average results for Queensland students in nearly all aspects of the tests were still below that of every other state and above only those for students in the Northern Territory.

Regional and remote areas of Queensland in particular did poorly, and plans were initiated by the Government to immediately address the apparent under-performance of students in the key areas of literacy and numeracy. Raising teacher expectations was seen as a central policy imperative. We were sceptical at that time of the apparent NAPLAN crisis for a number of reasons. In a submission to the Masters Review we argued that, if the demographic distinctiveness of Queensland was taken into account, then the NAPLAN results were equivalent to those of other States. Queensland had more regional and remote communities than States ranked higher on NAPLAN; it had a higher percentage of low socio-economic families, and it had a higher percentage of Aboriginal and Torres Strait Islander students than States ranked higher on NAPLAN. In addition, students in Queensland were younger on average than their interstate peers and had approximately one year less of schooling. Such appeals to contextual and local factors were dismissed in the final Masters Report as merely excuses for the failings of poor performing teachers and schools. We trace below how the deployment of a *teacher expectations* discourse in the McKinsey Report (Barber & Mourshed, 2007) and Masters Report (2009) shifted accountability for perceived under-performance squarely onto teachers and their expectations and standards.

The politics of expectations in the McKinsey Report

The emphasis given to high expectations in the Masters Report came directly from the McKinsey Report (Barber & Mourshed 2007), which purported to identify how the world's best-performing school systems come out on top of the global league tables. Excluded from the McKinsey Report, however, was any comparison or consideration of the actual pedagogy and curriculum of the systems. It is astonishing that variations in teaching and the actual content of curriculum could be disregarded as simply unimportant in such an influential review. Nonetheless, considerable attention was given to teachers' expectations, as well as the development of a culture of high expectations in schools. According to Barber and Mourshed (2007), systems should 'set high expectations for what each and every student should achieve; high expectations for what they know, understand and are able to do; [and] set high expectations for curriculum standards that establish high expectations for what students should achieve' (p.34). These expectations, Barber and Mourshed advised, should be benchmarked through strong accountability systems, notably by comparing performance between schools on national and international testing outcomes. Here we can discern the policy logic that treats test results as proxy measures for teachers' expectations. Raising performance seems to equate with simply insisting on higher expectations from teachers and high standards from students. The pedagogy and curriculum enabling these quality outcomes are left unexamined. McKinsey reduced the educational endeavour to a technical exercise of production where high expectations, high standards and quality control through constant monitoring and external testing were the only requirements.

The McKinsey Report was incredibly influential despite criticisms of its simplistic conclusions, its flawed methodology and its questionable ethics. As Coffield (2012, p.131) noted:

> Since the publication in September 2007 of the first McKinsey report, 'How the world's best-performing school systems come out on top', its conclusions have quickly hardened into new articles of faith for politicians, policy-makers, educational agencies and many researchers and practitioners, both in this country and abroad.

Regarding the ethics of the authors, Coffield (2012, p.137) pointed out that Michael Barber failed to declare a personal interest in his presentation of the statistics from England, where he was Chief Adviser to the Secretary of State for Education on school standards, and he failed to include any of the publicly available data which contradicted his claim that student outcomes in England had dramatically increased under his watch. Coffield (2012) contends that the undue influence of the McKinsey Report could be explained by the anxiety of politicians across the globe regarding how they could position their countries successfully in the global knowledge economy. When politicians are told authoritatively that positive transformation can be achieved, not by reforming their economy or modes of production, but by making rather simple changes to their schooling systems, including raising the expectations of teachers, then it is easy to understand the uptake of McKinsey's conclusions in policy documents. We would add that 'teachers' expectations' as an abstract and symbolic consideration for policy makers is a particularly attractive focus for reform because it requires little more than castigating teachers for not setting their standards higher. It is every politician's dream–an apparently effective form of large-scale intervention that requires no additional material resources. It also absolves politicians of any blame and shifts the accountability to teachers and their (apparently) low standards and expectations for student performance.

The politics of expectations in the Masters Report

Masters (2009) drew explicitly on the McKinsey Report throughout his review, and echoed core sentiments from its conclusions when reporting evidence on the features of high performing schools in Queensland. As the quotation below shows, central to high performance are the expectations that come via the principal–the high standards expected of teachers and students–and these are the object of continuous improvement and monitoring. The process of monitoring is not presented as a professional conversation between colleagues but as a top-down process of accountability where teachers are positioned as needing to account for the test performance of their students. The report states:

> In each of these high-performing schools, the principal … had high expectations of teachers and students and had put in place an effective leadership team with a shared commitment to continuous improvement.
>
> (Masters 2009, p.84)

A particular focus in the Masters Report was on the loaded word, 'excuse'. In successful schools, Masters (2009) noted, '*disadvantage is not used as an excuse for poor student outcomes*' (p.84). His comment appears initially as a laudable sentiment. In many ways it encapsulates our own critique of the deficit framing of disadvantaged students and the need to challenge low expectations of teachers. But in the context of the crisis around NAPLAN, 'excuse' operated as a discursive device to discount contextual and out-of-school factors in explaining students' test performance, and importantly it positioned individual teachers as personally accountable for students' learning, regardless of the context. Teachers who might want to offer explanations for students' test performance based on contextual considerations and local knowledge of students and their communities could be easily dismissed as simply looking for an excuse for their own failings. In commenting on high performing schools, Masters wrote:

> Underpinning the efforts of these schools appeared to be a belief that every student in the school was capable of successful learning and should be expected to demonstrate progress. The fact that a school was in a socioeconomically disadvantaged area was not seen by the principal as an acceptable excuse for reduced expectations.
>
> (p.85)

'Not an acceptable excuse' positions teachers as already guilty. There is no 'excuse' for poor test performance! At this time, principals and teachers in apparently under-performing schools in Queensland were vulnerable and shamed, and expressed their response to the mandated school audits following NAPLAN in vivid and emotional terms, such as 'feeling naked and exposed' (Brennan, Zipin & Sellar 2016). A common response from many principals who came to audit their 'under-performing' schools was to invite them to 'come walk in my shoes' and observe the professional work that they did with students and families in this region (Brennan, Zipin & Sellar 2016).

The discourse around teacher expectations following Masters, therefore, became part of a reductive discourse of top-down accountability where schools and teachers had to be closely monitored, and student performance constantly assessed, primarily through national testing regimes like NAPLAN. Engagement with a multifaceted curriculum and worthwhile learning in relation to cognitive, affective and civic outcomes (Biesta 2007) was sidelined in favour of performance measures on tests. It is pertinent, therefore, to highlight the following extract from Masters (2009), where the word 'performance' has replaced the notion of 'learning':

> A commitment to high expectations was accompanied in these schools by a deep interest in how well these expectations were being achieved. The principal and other members of the senior leadership team analysed, discussed and shared with staff evidence about student performance, including comparisons of the school's results over time and with state-wide data.
>
> (p.86)

Teachers are positioned here in this text in a hierarchical relationship with the principal who performs the analysis of the test results for them and shares evidence about how they are performing. The replacement of *learning* by *performance* is an important discursive marker of the nature of the policies introduced after the Masters Report. Principals and their staff became more preoccupied with performativity as they sought direct ways to improve test results and maintain their own appearance and status as successful professionals within the schooling system.

High expectations framed by performativity and accountability

There is an eerie absence in the McKinsey and Masters Reports of the actual experience of teachers and students in classrooms. Classrooms are places of multifaceted, complex and close relationships. Every teacher can tell stories of worrying about specific students, of sharing emotionally charged experiences with their classes and of caring about individuals and groups of students. This *particularity* is at the heart of differentiated teaching and the notion of high expectations. Especially in regional towns and cities like those where Red Point High was situated, teachers are part of the community and are recognised and regularly acknowledged by parents and students in shopping centres and recreation venues. We present this image of the embodied and lived experience of teaching and learning to create a point of contrast with the technical and reductionist framing of quality teaching that is proffered in the two influential reports by McKinsey and Masters. Reflect on how you might complete the following sentence: *A commitment to high expectations was accompanied in these schools by a deep interest in. . . .* A deep interest in what or whom? A social justice framing of high expectations, we contend, would focus on particular students and groups of students, their funds of knowledge and cultural resources, their interests, their challenges, their families and communities, as well as their cultural and political positioning in the society. So in brief, our word to complete the sentence would be *students, a deep interest in students.* A neo-liberal perspective focusses instead on issues of performativity. The deep interest privileged by Masters is 'evidence about student performance, including comparisons of the school's results over time and with state-wide data' (Masters 2009, p.86). In brief, his completion of the cloze comprehension exercise is *performance or data*. This neo-liberal and performative framing of teaching entered persuasively into the conversations between teachers and principals across Queensland following the Masters Report.

Teachers at Red Point High were necessarily aware of, and implicated in the process of 'datafication' (Lingard, Thompson & Sellar 2016; Ozga 2009) of their professional practices. Datafication throughout the whole system of schooling had been achieved through the implementation of NAPLAN, the establishment of the MySchool website that provided public comparative metrics on all schools in Australia and through state-wide published audits of the performance of all schools. But teachers at Red Point High were not simply conduits for the neo-liberal discourse of performativity and datafication that was driving policy initiatives locally and globally. Some teachers continued to draw upon enduring professional discourses of fairness and care to constitute their distinctive positions. Other teachers expressed elitist and exclusionary discourses to question where the school was headed under the leadership of Phil, the new principal.

We turn now to examine in detail the way these discourses intersected in teachers' notions of high expectations. In the following analyses we foreground interviews with Phil, who was particularly concerned with the quality of pedagogy in the lowest streamed classes at the school. The Indigenous liaison worker, Aileen, also voiced concern about streaming for Indigenous students, and so her interviews are drawn upon. More broadly the kinds of expectations held by teachers are noted, as well as the viewpoint of Kath, the deputy principal. As we noted in introducing this chapter, there was widespread use of 'expectations' by teachers at Red Point High to elaborate the defining culture of the school. Here we draw out the tensions and contradictions in this discourse to reveal the political nature of differentiation.

Politics of admission at Red Point High

Red Point High, we realised soon after beginning our interviews, had an established reputation of being a high performing academic school for bright students. It was the preferred school for many families in the city. It also had an enrolment management plan that enabled students to be admitted on a merit basis into programs of 'academic excellence' and 'excellence in performing arts and music'.

Merit-based enrolment policies created an aura of high standards and high expectations that reinforced the reputation of Red Point High. However, in the discourses that circulated at the school around the admission policy, a point of conflict emerged between the principal and some teachers who opposed his welcoming of Indigenous participation in the school and his official acknowledgement of Indigenous custodianship of the land on which Red Point High was built. He confessed that some teachers worried he might be turning Red Point High into a 'Black school' (see Chapter 4):

> . . . it's a little bit challenging for some people, and I've sensed some raised eyebrows when I acknowledge the Indigenous . . . yeah don't worry it wasn't lost on me [laughs] I know, some people are like, what's he doing? . . . what's he going to do, he's going to turn it into a Black school, you know, like, all the Indigenous kids are going to come here now. Well, I mean, if there are people with that attitude I'd be really, I'm troubled by that, and they need to take a good look at themselves. 'Cause in the end, on face value, when you get up and say I'd like to acknowledge the traditional owners of the land, anyone who's sitting there saying that's rubbish is clearly . . . [laughs]
>
> (Phil)

Clearly what? Phil never names racism as the underlying reason for some of the staff objecting to his acknowledging the Indigenous elders and questioning the increasing number of Indigenous students at the school. We might reasonably make that inference regarding racism based on the long history of institutional racism in Australia towards Indigenous people. Rather, Phil presented a more sympathetic explanation for some teachers' opposition to Indigenous enrolments and acknowledgement. He suggested that they were not prepared for the challenges of teaching more students in the lower streams. He explained that Indigenous students typically are streamed into the lowest groups and present a particular pedagogical challenge for teachers accustomed to dealing with academically able White students:

> Yeah, with 1500 kids, actually I think it's less than 5 per cent (Indigenous), I think it's about 4 per cent (Indigenous). It's still . . . it's a low percentage but, unfortunately, because of the statistical reality that those kids often are low literacy and numeracy, they are tended to be grouped into classes, you know, because classes are streamed, so they end up in a group, you know, so there's that factor. And that's probably more challenging for teachers that haven't been used to [it] in the past. And I think we need a greater level of support around those kids.

The politics of admission at Red Point High on the one hand involved maintaining and enhancing the reputation of the school as having high standards and expectations. On the other hand, the implementation of the admission policy under the previous principal seemed to limit the enrolment of Indigenous students whereas under Phil's leadership Indigenous enrolments were increasing. Some teachers now worried about the reputation of Red Point High if it was to be perceived as a 'Black school'. The politics of admission, therefore, pitted White privilege, expressed in apparently neutral terms as upholding high expectations and standards, against social justice concerns about becoming a more inclusive school that welcomed and supported students from the Indigenous community. During the period of our research project, this struggle over the identity of the school as 'Black' or 'traditional with high expectations' continued as an undercurrent of tension between Phil and some teachers, rather than an explicit professional dialogue in the school about race and privilege and the role of the school in the city as supporting a social justice agenda. This tension around Indigeneity also played out in discourses regarding streaming.

Politics of streaming at Red Point High

When asked if the school-wide endorsement of high expectations was working for Aboriginal and Torres Strait Islander students, the Indigenous liaison worker, Aileen, explained the negative effects of streaming on their engagement at the school:

> Because when I came in here, you know, they were streamed, and all the lows were there and that's what you're expected to do, you know.

She summarised the effect of streaming as 'not good' because:

> They feel that they're all stupid. They don't really know much so they don't really try, you know. And this year I'm hearing from up there the expectations are . . . you know, we've gotta look at higher expectations from the kids.

This mention of 'higher expectations from the kids' repeats almost exactly the sentiment expressed by Barber and Mourshed (2007) and Masters (2009) that raising achievement outcomes in schools simply requires 'expecting higher standards from students'. However, the feedback to the Indigenous students from the policy of streaming, as these comments from Aileen suggest, affected their collective identity (*'they feel they're all stupid'*), their sense of having relevant knowledge (*'they don't really know much'*) and their motivation to try (*'so they don't really try'*). These are powerful negative messages that research has shown undermine students' motivation to learn (Hattie & Timperley 2007). As Aileen notes, the expectations 'from the kids' are not high enough according to 'up there', which is a reference to the principal and his leadership team at the school. The expectations discourse at Red Point High according to Aileen focuses on the deficits of students, rather than the inadequate pedagogies that are deployed by teachers in low-streamed classes.

Phil's own evaluation of the actual practice of streaming at Red Point High is in complete agreement with Aileen's views. He personally monitored the quality of teaching in high-, medium- and low-streamed classes to determine whether all classes were being taught in a manner that conveys high expectations:

> I think one of the interesting things is, I did this . . . I try and get round to some classes as much as I can and I went and visited, you know, I looked on the timetable and found, like, a top level maths class, a middle of the road, and a lower level, and just to go look at the different . . . and think, well, what does high expectations look like. Well, in the top and to be fair the middle it was high expectations, I mean, the kids really, you know, working well and really engaged, but in the lower stream class just basically, you know, the expectation around academic achievement was almost non-existent. The only expectations were around, you know, keeping the kids quiet you know, there's some teachers that must surely know that they're not really delivering on high expectations.

Phil's view that kids in the bottom streams were simply being 'kept quiet' supports Aileen's assessment of the poor quality teaching offered to Indigenous students in the bottom streams, but the focus of reform, as noted above, was on lifting the students' expectations as if they were the source of the problem rather than the structures deployed by the school itself.

A teacher we interviewed on the first day weighed the benefits and drawbacks of streaming, noting that it concentrates students with behavioural problems into one space and makes effective teaching more difficult:

> When you've got the behaviour problem classes, you know, sometimes if you had a few more of those better kids it might influence those ones to pick up their game and, you know, be a positive influence that way. So, I think streaming and not streaming has its advantages and disadvantages. It works sometimes and then other times it's probably better that it didn't happen.
>
> (Lenore)

While she didn't name Indigeneity as the issue, Lenore's view is consistent with the view of Phil and Aileen that concentrating disengaged and perhaps alienated students into low-streamed classes created a challenge for teachers that seemed at times beyond their skills, or perhaps for some teachers at the school, beyond their will and motivation to engage proactively with the challenge.

To conclude this section on the politics of streaming, we highlight again that key members of staff at Red Point High were concerned about the negative effects of streaming on some students, particularly Indigenous students, but nobody at the school suggested it should be discarded or gradually phased out.

Politics of academic expectations: Value adding

We noted above that the politics of admission to Red Point High pivoted on privileging academic excellence while orchestrating the exclusion of students who might struggle to perform academically. The racist discourse underlying the admission policy was noted also in the undercurrent of negative comments from some teachers about Red Point High becoming a '*Black school*' if too many Indigenous students were enrolled. In this section we identify a set of similar discourses that played out in the politics of academic expectations at Red Point High. The first relates to the neo-liberal discourse of treating students as products in a marketplace. The neo-liberal school is imagined as a production space where 'value is added' and 'relative gains' are measured and graphed. Data are crucial in this neo-liberal discourse of value-added production, so schools, including Red Point High, have become much more data savvy, and typically appoint a qualified teacher as a data analyst to interpret tests and other performance data and communicate key implications to the school administrative staff and teachers. Teachers are appraised in terms of their 'value-adding' to students' performance. These fine-grained quantitative comparisons are used at Red Point High to guard against teachers becoming complacent. No longer is it sufficient that teachers have achieved 'great results' (as mentioned in Chapter 2), as the principal says, but the school has to be seen as value-adding in significant ways.

Many teachers have been at Red Point High for lengthy periods of time, and it has maintained a strong reputation across the generations for academic performance. Phil used the discourse of the market to challenge any complacency amongst staff, especially in terms of high performing students:

> I've done some stuff with the staff showing them the relative gain on NAPLAN, so showing them from grade 7 to 9 how much relative gain the students actually had here. And that was a bit of an eye opener for the teachers cause they were a bit blown away to see that the relative gain is actually not really good here. . . .

The value-added discourse created a tool for Phil to push teachers to expect more and achieve more with their students. High academic expectations were now a matter of teachers seeking to achieve continual improvement that can be chartered by graphs of relative gain over time and relative performance to other schools.

The discourse of high academic expectations at Red Point High, however, marginalised students who struggled at school. Struggling students were seen by Phil as problematic due to the systemic failure of the school to follow up and deal with their real needs:

> It's a high expectation school and, you know, it's clearly that way, it's academic, but my concern is, yeah, there are kids who are obviously struggling, and because they're struggling they become behaviour management issues.

The very presence of struggling students is a challenge to the reputation of Red Point High as an academic school. These students are positioned on the periphery of the school; they appear marginal to Phil, whose own evaluation of their classes indicated a pedagogy of neglect (*'being kept quiet'*) and a behaviour management regime that processes them efficiently (*'basically being processed, like through the mill'*) but doesn't really address their needs:

> They're, sort of, being processed in terms of behaviour management, (basically being processed, like through the mill), but I'm not sure if we're really addressing their source needs in why they ended up being a behaviour management issue in the first place. To me, I think there needs to be a better coordination around the whole, sort of, tracking of student service to, you know, the kids falling through the cracks sort of stuff.

The principal's comments reveal the contest at Red Point High between neo-liberal discourses of the market (value-adding) and meritocracy (academic school) and caring discourses about struggling students who are marginalised. He is concerned about all students at Red Point High and contrasts the high academic reputation of the school as a place for 'bright kids' with the neglected needs of struggling students that this meritocratic discourse marginalises.

Politics of behavioural expectations

Red Point High had developed an integrated program of behaviour management that teachers valued and students understood. For example, in response to the question, *What's it like to teach here?*, a teacher responded as follows:

> I can't even imagine going anywhere else. I'm extremely happy here. You get support from Admin and the leadership team, particularly in terms of behaviour. You know that the kids know that if they go to Admin, that means something. It's certainly a choice that they weigh up. You say, 'You're making this choice. Are you sure you want to do that?' Whereas in other schools, you feel like it's what you do, and what you do alone, that you can rely on.
>
> (Nicola)

The whole school approach to behaviour management had established a shared culture of high standards regarding students' behaviour. The following explores the features of these high standards and how they related to social justice and differentiation.

The teachers' discourses on behavioural expectations consistently privileged compliance with conventional norms regarding uniforms and the outward appearance of the school. A view expressed by one teacher captured this tone of compliance and uniformity quite vividly:

> We've got quite a stringent uniform–I know it's a public school and so forth, but we've got quite a stringent uniform. I tell you what–if you go to a swimming carnival, and your school is the only one in uniform–it develops a sense of pride. As much as the kids don't like the rules they're given, it does develop a sense of pride. The kids can see that they're all together–this is [Red Point High]–and then there are these other schools.
>
> (Helen)

The deputy principal, Kath, echoed this sentiment when noting that the distinctiveness of Red Point High was:

> . . . its traditional flavour. We're strict on the basics and things that affect the outward image of the school, like uniform and discipline.

There were numerous other comments from teachers that supported this description of the school culture as traditional, compliance oriented and requiring uniformity. The words and phrases that they used included 'boundaries are clear', 'consistent from the start' and 'you can't start weak'.

High standards linked to student compliance can become an authoritarian stance, as revealed in the comment below, where the Welfare Officer, Cassandra, regretted the stance of some teachers who expected students to just be there and listen to what they say. She wondered why these teachers were still teaching:

> I think there are teachers who just want to get on with the job, and not worry too much about the relationship side of it, 'The kids must just be there and do what I say, and that's it'. But if they understand, it would make their job more satisfying if they can get to know the kids a little better. Maybe some of our teachers need a change. I don't know why they're doing the job!

The discourse about high standards and behaviour management did create tensions between those teachers (such as Cassandra) who regarded relationships with students as foundational to effective management versus teachers who treated the management regime at Red Point High as a set of rules that students needed to obey, no questions asked.

In summary, the teachers' discourses regarding high expectations for academic achievement and behavioural standards are consistent with the neo-liberal privileging of performativity and accountability. National testing and other accountability technologies have made schools like Red Point High highly sensitive to their public appearance, as well as the importance of elite academic performance and the requirement for teachers to 'value add' in ways that can be measured and communicated publically. So high expectations operates as an objectifying discourse that creates a constant pressure on teachers not to be complacent and to expect even better performance from students, especially the elite students. With regard to the lower-streamed students, the interview with Phil revealed a sense of regret that more couldn't be done for them, 'it's a high expectation school and, you know, it's clearly that way, it's academic, but my concern is, yeah, there are kids who are obviously struggling'. Struggling academically at Red Point High seemed to bring into question students' identity as legitimate members of the school–they are kids who don't fit with the high academic expectations. Not only did they struggle academically; that struggle led to behavioural non-compliance and further marginalisation. But this is not the whole story. There was a contesting discourse we picked up from Cassandra and Phil about relating to students, getting to know students, caring about the students and addressing their 'source needs'. This kind of relational pedagogy replaces 'knowing students' through their academic performance profiles, test scores or disciplinary sanctions ('blue slips') with knowing students as embodied persons with aspirations and interests and possibilities beyond their current circumstances. This counter discourse on caring about and relating to students is explored further in the following chapter.

Conclusion

The discourses deployed by the teachers at Red Point High regarding high expectations reveal a complex and contested terrain with regard to the politics of differentiation. First, an exclusionary politics of differentiation can be discerned with regard to admission to the school. High expectations discourses had been deployed for some time at Red Point High to maintain a White middle class clientele of academically able students. The racial aspect of this enrolment policy was revealed when Phil overheard backchat from long-term staff members at the school who complained that he seemed intent on turning Red Point High into a 'Black school', because he was allowing more enrolment from the Indigenous community and recognising their culture and custodianship of the land by formal acknowledgement during whole school gatherings. He also had asked for an additional flagpole to be installed so that separate Aboriginal and Torres Strait Islander flags could be flown in front of the school along with the National flag. These important steps to recognise the place of Indigenous students within the school created resentment and concern amongst some staff. Naming racism as the basis of this reaction, however, posed difficulties for Phil. Racism invokes a harsh ethical and moral judgement of other teachers, and Phil preferred to regard their back-chat comments and resistance to Indigenous enrolments as related to a lack of professional knowledge and skill regarding how to teach low performing students. His observations of the quality of the pedagogy in the low streams suggested it was a pedagogy of indifference (Lingard & Keddie 2013) designed to keep students quiet rather than engage and extend their knowledge.

Within the school, a disabling politics of differentiation operated with regard to streaming. It is apparent that Indigenous students at Red Point High were expected to struggle, and in fact the streaming practices at the school concentrated them in the lower streams. Aileen, the Indigenous liaison worker, spoke passionately about the negative effects on students of such low expectations in these streamed classes and the sense of failure and low motivation that it engrained in students. She confronted this pedagogy of indifference and discrimination with emotional engagement and daily support for her Indigenous students, and she sought ways to personally guide them through difficult times. However, she did not explicitly challenge the politics of streaming. She was unhappy and critical, but when moving from critique of the school to describing her own strategy, she shifted to an individualistic focus of building up particular students' resilience and supporting them to succeed within the current practices of the school. She wanted greater support from the school for her work, and she wanted greater recognition as a highly valued member of the administrative team, but neither she nor Phil sought to reform the streaming approach to differentiation that so clearly disadvantaged Indigenous students and others in the low streams.

A proactive politics is required to address these ingrained practices within the school. An explicit professional dialogue was necessary at Red Point High to address the intersection of issues of race, expectations and oppressive forms of differentiation. It is apparent that the high expectations discourses that circulated at Red Point High provided a safe and neutral terrain where difficult issues could be avoided. Everyone could endorse high expectations but actually signify a host of conflicting positions. For some staff high expectations seemed to refer mainly to performativity and the external image of the school to the local community. The wearing of a consistent school uniform and being seen in public as orderly and conformist were salient for many of the teachers. For some teachers high expectations related to behaviour codes and school rules, and this focus justified a view amongst some teachers that it was not their role to get to know students or investigate their interests. Rather students needed to step up and meet the high behavioural and academic expectations or leave the school.

In the next chapter we foreground the emotional dimensions of differentiated teaching through an analysis of the discourses of care and solidarity at Red Point High. We suggest that teachers' everyday interactions with students challenge the 'eerie absence' of care that characterised the technical and reductionist framings of quality teaching in recent reports (Masters 2009; McKinsey 2007). In contrast to this technical framing of teaching, we highlight the stories of concern and worry that teachers express for specific groups of students as well as individuals in their classrooms, their accounts of emotionally charged experiences with students and the intense care they offer to specific students. Our interviews include quite intense stories of personal investment by teachers in trying to negotiate new identities for the students and mediating new relationships between the students, the school and their parents. What we offer then is a view of social justice that foregrounds affective justice and the challenge of caring for students in a differentiated manner.

References

Barber, M & Mourshed, M 2007, *How the world's best performing school systems come out on top*, McKinsey & Company, New York.

Biesta, G 2007, 'Why "what works" won't work: Evidence-based practice and the democratic deficit in educational research', *Educational Theory*, Vol. 57, no. 1, pp. 1–22.

Brennan, M, Zipin, L, & Sellar, S 2016, 'Negotiating with neighbours: Balancing different accountabilities across a cluster of regional schools', In *National Testing in Schools: An Australian Assessment*, ed B Lingard, G Thompson, & S Sellar, Routledge, Abingdon OX, pp.199–211.

Brophy, JE 1983, 'Research on the self-fulfilling prophecy and teacher expectations', *Journal of Educational Psychology*, Vol. 75, no. 5, pp. 631–661.

Brophy, JE & Good, TL 1972, 'Teacher expectations: Beyond the Pygmalion controversy', *Phi Delta Kappan*, Vol. 54, no. 4, pp. 276–278.

Coffield, F 2012, 'Why the McKinsey reports will not improve school systems', *Journal of Education Policy*, Vol. 27, no. 1, pp. 131–149.

Comber, B 2016, *Literacy place and pedagogies of possibility*, Routledge, New York.

Connell, R 1993, Schools and social justice. Philadelphia, Temple University Press.

Eder, D 1981, 'Ability grouping as a self-fulfilling prophecy: A micro-analysis of teacher-student interaction', *Sociology of Education*, Vol. 54, no. 3, pp. 151–162.

Fraser, N 1997, *Justice interruptus: Critical reflections on the 'postsocialist' condition*, Routledge, New York.

Fraser, N 2009, *Scales of justice: Reimagining political space in a globalizing world*, Columbia University Press, New York.

Good, TL 1987, 'Two decades of research on teacher expectations: Findings and future directions', *Journal of Teacher Education*, Vol. 38, no. 4, pp. 32–47.

Hattie, J & Timperley, H 2007, 'The power of feedback', *Review of educational research*, Vol. 77, no. 1, pp. 81–112.

Ireson, J, Hallam, S, & Hurley, C 2005, 'What are the effects of ability grouping on GCSE attainment?', *British Educational Research Journal*, Vol. 31, no. 4, pp. 443–458.

Lingard, B & Keddie, A 2013, 'Redistribution and recognition: Working against pedagogies of indifference', *Pedagogy, Culture and Society*, Vol. 21, no. 3, pp. 427–447.

Lingard, B, Thompson, G, & Sellar, S (eds) 2016, *National testing in schools: An Australian assessment*, Routledge, Abingdon Oxford.

Masters, G 2009, *A shared challenge: Improving literacy, numeracy and science learning in Queensland primary schools*, Australian Council for Educational Research, Melbourne.

McNaughton, S & Mei Kuin Lai 2008, *A model of school change for culturally and linguistically diverse students in New Zealand: A summary and evidence from systematic replication*, Woolf Fisher Research Centre, University of Auckland.

Mehan, H 1992, 'Understanding inequality in schools: The contribution of interpretive studies', *Sociology of Education*, Vol. 65, no. 1, pp. 1–20.

Ozga, J 2009,' Governing education through data in England: From regulation to self-evaluation', *Journal of Education Policy*, Vol. 24, no. 2, pp. 149–162.

Rist, R 1970, 'Student social class and teacher expectations: The self-fulfilling prophecy in ghetto education', *Harvard Educational Review*, Vol. 40, no. 3, pp. 411–451.

Rosenthal, R & Jacobson, L 1968, *Pygmalion in the classroom: Teacher expectation and pupil's intellectual ability*, Rinehart & Winston, New York.

Sahlberg, P 2011, *Finnish lessons*, Teachers College Press, New York.

Sarra, C 2005, *Strong and smart: Reinforcing aboriginal perspectives of being aboriginal at Cherbourg State School.* PhD thesis, Murdoch University, Perth.

Sarra, C 2008, 'School accountability: Asking some overdue hard questions', *Indigenous Education Leadership Institute*, Caboolture, Qld.

Sarra, C 2011, *Strong and smart–towards a pedagogy for emancipation: Education for first peoples.* Abingdon, Oxon: Routledge.

Sorhagen, NS 2013, 'Early teacher expectations disproportionately affect poor children's high school performance', *Journal of Educational Psychology*, Vol. 105, no. 2, pp. 465–477.

Stronger Smarter Institute Limited 2014, *High-expectations relationships: A foundation for quality learning environments in all Australian schools.* Stronger Smarter Institute, Caboolture, Qld.

Zipin, L 2009, 'Dark funds of knowledge, deep funds of pedagogy: Exploring boundaries between lifeworlds and schools', *Discourse: Studies in the Cultural Politics of Education*, Vol. 30, no. 3, pp. 317–331.

4 A politics of differentiation and care

The plight of refugees fleeing war and persecution has recently dominated the political agenda in Europe and the UK as well as in Australia. As part of Australia's border protection regime, refugees who attempt to arrive in the country by boat are either returned to their country of origin, imprisoned in off-shore detention centres or have their boats turned around. They are told they will never be permitted to enter Australia. This policy has received bi-partisan support from the two major Australian political parties, despite condemnation from the United Nations. Central to the arguments posited by both parties in defending this policy has been that they care for refugees and do not want to see them drowning at sea, as has happened in the past, and that such draconian policies are necessary to deter people from making dangerous journeys to Australia. Care operates as an exclusionary device to keep people out 'for their own good'. Whilst perhaps not as dramatic or as punitive, many of the uses of the term 'care' in schools reflect a similar concern to patrol the borders of the school in order that only deserving students are able to enrol; but once enrolled then 'care' is offered to ensure compliance with school expectations. Teachers and school administrators demonstrate care by being 'tough' on students for their own good (encapsulated in the term 'tough love'); they demonstrate a care for the image of the school (and ostensibly the 'good' students who attend it) by excluding students who might damage its reputation; and they demonstrate 'care' for their curriculum subjects by adopting gatekeeper approaches that deny access to certain students who are likely to undermine its 'standards'. The parallel between the political discourses of caring for refugees and caring for students highlights the contradictory and perverse ways that 'care' might be deployed to justify distancing and objectifying practices. On the other hand, during our research we noted that teachers deployed 'care' to challenge such objectifying practices and to foreground ethical and emotional engagement with students' lives at school and beyond. We turn now to elaborate on these contesting notions of care in relation to the politics of differentiation.

When we were writing the chapter on the politics of teacher expectations at Red Point High, we became increasingly aware of the ways in which a politics of care was implicated within these expectations. Care was officially embedded in Red Point High's own vision statement, and the teachers spoke about caring when they expressed concerns about academic excellence, behavioural standards and the reputation of the school within the local community. The official school care agenda could be experienced by students as 'harsh', as one of the students told us in an interview. However, talking with teachers we also heard stories from them about wanting to know their students better in order to support them emotionally when times were tough. There were also instances of caring about specific groups, as demonstrated by the flagpole incident, where care was symbolised through the efforts of the Indigenous liaison worker and the principal to install an extra flagpole to display both the Aboriginal *and* Torres Strait Islander flags at the front of the school. The politics framing these aspects of schooling at Red Point High highlighted the significant, but oftentimes fraught, process of caring for students and prompted conversations amongst ourselves about what it means to care within a school. This inevitably led us to a discussion about the politics of care in relation to differentiation.

Some of our discussion focussed on how much of the care discourse was concerned with performative forms of caring, that is, worrying about the public representation and appearance of the school, its academic reputation and the visible order of the school. Other discussions focused on whether an ethic of critical care was implicated in the way teachers supported students' academic achievement through a combination of social support and high expectations involving cajoling and pushing students to achieve better results (see Ladson-Billings 1995). There were also telling comments from teachers about caring personally for particular students, of being invested in ensuring the student's emotional wellbeing and of seeking to understand the student's home-life, interests and aspirations. Such personalised care is a form of differentiation that places affective wellbeing at the centre of the teachers' work. In trying to make sense of these different discourses on care, we were drawn to Kathleen Lynch's (2012) distinctions between love, care and solidarity and their relationship to social justice. As with other feminist scholars (Blackmore 1999; 2006; Boler 1999; Hochschild 1983; Noddings 1988), Lynch challenges the privileging of rationality and the public sphere in how knowledge and citizenship are valued and constructed. She positions this privileging as trivialising and silencing relational matters of care and thus as eschewing the importance of the affective domain in understandings of social justice. She explains that: '. . . affective inequality occurs directly when people are deprived of the love, care and solidarity they need to survive and develop as human beings and/or when they are abused, violated or neglected affectively' (p.3). Such a notion resonated for us in the stories we were hearing from teachers about some of the deprivation students at Red Point High were grappling with in their out-of-school lives, the impact of such deprivation on their capacity to engage with school and the teachers' struggles to address such deprivation.

In relation to Lynch's notion of solidarity, Aileen, the Indigenous liaison worker at Red Point High, clearly enacted caring in solidarity with the Indigenous students at the school. Her practices were consistent with Chris Sarra's (2003; 2008) Indigenous education philosophy of Strong and Smart (mentioned in the previous chapter). This sense of care for Indigenous students is grounded in valuing their Indigenous identity within the school (*strong*) and creating realistic expectations that they should achieve as well as non-Indigenous students (*smart*). This philosophy exemplifies 'solidarity'–a concern for the injustices that have been perpetrated against a social group and the emotional costs of that. As a matter of working towards affective equality, we take up this notion later in the chapter in further exploring some of the issues at Red Point High confronting Indigenous students.

In foregrounding the emotional dimensions of differentiated teaching in this chapter, we also seek to counter the 'eerie absence' of care mentioned in the previous chapter in relation to the technical and reductionist framings of quality teaching in reports such as those by Barber and Mourshed (2007) and Masters (2009). In contrast to this technical framing of teaching, we highlight the stories of concern and worry that teachers express for specific groups of students as well as individuals in their classrooms, their accounts of emotionally charged experiences with students and the intense care they offer to specific students. Theirs, importantly, is a focus predominantly on learning rather than performance. These quite intense stories recount personal investment by teachers in trying to negotiate new identities for the students and mediating new relationships between the students, the school and their parents. We draw on the voices of 'Phil' (the Principal), 'Kath' (the Deputy Principal), 'Aileen' (Indigenous Liaison worker), 'Cassandra' (Welfare Officer), teachers ('Larissa', 'Fiona', 'Charlie', 'Pamela', 'Karen' and 'Lenore') and students ('Dan', 'Nigel', 'Celina' and 'Olivia') in this chapter to examine a number of instances where this kind of personal care was revealed in our interviews with teachers. The stories in this chapter will be familiar to many who work in schools. What we offer here is a way of interpreting such stories in terms of how social justice is constrained and limited through particular understandings of care, and how we might see justice more broadly in relation to care and differentiation.

Caring for Red Point High in a differentiated market

In order to compete within current performative cultures of schooling, individual schools need to differentiate themselves from their competitors. In this climate there is no room for the 'ordinary school' (Maguire et al. 2011). As such, high on the agenda of school administrators is the 'fabrication' of a reputation that will ensure the school can attract a high percentage of the 'market share' of students (Keddie et al. 2011). The concern is with the 'right' kind of students, that is, those who will enhance the school's reputation and attract similar students. This has led to schools focusing on enhancing, retaining or improving their academic reputation, sometimes through designer programs to attract high performing students, or by excluding those students likely to damage that reputation (Mills, Renshaw & Zipin 2013). However, in the vast majority of schools, there is a concern beyond the academic standing of the school to include the construction of the school as a 'caring' place. This care relates to both the way in which the school will have high expectations of all students in terms of their academic efforts and behaviours, and the way in which teachers will look out for the emotional and physical welfare of their students. Being a caring school is good for business.

A rationalist sense of care (Lynch 2012) was central to Red Point High's positioning within the marketplace of competing schools. It had an established reputation of being a high performing academic school for 'bright' students. This reputation had been exclusionary, as we noted in the previous chapter, particularly in relation to Indigenous students, exemplified in many teachers' fears that the relaxing of its enrolment policy may lead to damaging its exemplary academic reputation. The reputation was policed through various mechanisms to ensure that the 'right people' enrolled in the school. The local community was largely middle class, and Red Point High's enrolment policy ensured that students could not be 'bussed in' from outside the catchment area. However, due to its excellence programs, exceptions could be made for 'high performers' from outside that area. Maintaining this reputation was something that teachers really 'cared' about. Such care can be read in many ways. For example, it can be read as caring for the students who were already enrolled in the school and maintaining standards so the capital accrued for those attending Red Point High was not eroded. It could also be read as maintaining the status of the teachers as high quality performers achieving excellent results. It could also be read as a way of ensuring that the community of the school remains cohesive by not including anyone who would not fit in. In this latter regard we are reminded of Zygmunt Bauman's (2001) warnings about the danger of 'community'. A community can only exist when there are outsiders–those who do not belong. In this sense, caring about the school community is linked to an exclusionary logic–we exclude because we care.

Exclusion is a strong word, evoking feelings of anger and resentment in those excluded and requiring a strong moral case to be articulated by those proposing the policy of exclusion. In trying to be more inclusive of Indigenous students at the school, for example, the principal heard mutterings among some staff about him trying to undermine Red Point High's established reputation. However, the principal did not directly engage with this kind of exclusionary resistance from staff. Rather he rationalised their resistance as related to a lack of skill, a technical deficiency in the staff, not a moral failing. He explained to us that the teachers tended not to be prepared for the challenges of teaching 'lower ability' students, as they were accustomed to dealing with academic students. Thus, the 'care' discourses about protecting the school's identity and reputation for academic excellence operated as a cover for excluding students who might have benefitted greatly from the resources offered by the school.

Being part of a community evokes warm sentiments regarding a sense of belonging, of feeling safe and of forming relationships that are built on trust and mutual interests. But membership comes at a cost. With belonging also comes the requirement to accept the values and ethos of the community and comply with community practices. At Red Point High when compliance was not evident in students, a caring 're-education' was deployed. The re-education regime, despite entailing punitive practices and being seen as 'harsh' by some, was interpreted by many students as the school caring about them. This is perhaps not surprising, given the effort that the school had put into developing institutional forms of care. One of the clearest expressions of the school's efforts to frame itself around notions of care came from the teacher who was the designated welfare officer at the school. She told us about her role in the following terms:

> I tend to work with the Year level co-ordinators to make sure they've got the strategic direction in terms of care, and dealing with a lot of those Admin areas. I've also been involved in developing our care expectations.
>
> (Cassandra)

The school's practices regarding care are familiar in most schools, and included: following up consistently on particular students' progress; working with parents and guardians to assist students in practical ways to complete assignments; explicitly addressing bullying episodes in a timely way; and investing time outside the classroom to get to know the students. The efficiency and pragmatism of this form of institutional care was made clear when Kath, the deputy principal, invited us to observe how non-compliant students who had received a 'blue slip' during the day for poor behaviour or for failing to complete homework were forced to catch up on work at lunchtime. Whilst representing a small percentage of the school's student population, it was clear that quite a few students struggled to accept the school ethos and so entered into various forms of re-education. This sense of caring was further articulated by Kath in her focus on habit formation and the development of self-regulation in students. We explore this form of re-education further below. Despite such punitive measures in response to non-compliance, our sense in the interviews with students was that they felt the teachers and the school generally cared about them:

> Um, it's [the school] organised. Like, some other schools aren't as organised as we are. The teachers, like, care for you more.
>
> (Dan)

> They're harsh but fair. They really do care but they're not going to, you know, make it hell for us, not too strict. But they do take an interest. If you're going to mess up all the time, they're going to do something about it.
>
> (Nigel)

Care discourses at Red Point High drew upon performativity concerns that privileged the maintenance of visible order. The care experienced by the students was important to them, but somewhat distant and related to institutional tidiness–'we're organised', and 'they're going to do something about it (messing up)'. The students we interviewed, nonetheless, valued this kind of care within a friendly and supportive environment. When we asked them what was the best thing about Red Point High, they quickly pointed to the high level of support from teachers and fellow students:

> The people, most of them are friendly . . . the kids and the teachers help you to get everything right, like, to do the best in your exams.
>
> (Celina)

> Um, they take the education really seriously. They really want you to do well, so, I think that's really good.
>
> (Olivia)

The comments by the two students above illustrated the performative expectations of care at Red Point High–a care discourse that emphasises examination results, doing well and getting everything correct. The message to the students is that 'we care about your behaviour' and 'we care about your educational success'. Affective care for the whole person in the current moment is subsumed by the rationalist sense of care for the students as achieving learners at school and successful employees in the future.

As noted above, a key practice implemented by Kath was caring for the students by instilling compliant behavioural habits and self-regulation to ensure success at Red Point High, as she explained:

> We're insistent that every kid does their assessment, so even if it's past the due by date we don't say, well too bad you've missed out. There's an expectation that they will be kept in by the teacher's aide, you know, 20 minutes over their lunch time until they have completed it. The seniors actually get suspended or put in the [withdrawal] room if they don't do it, and the juniors certainly are as well.

Insisting on every student completing assessment was an important focus at Red Point towards students fulfilling the requirements for graduation. This was certainly not a laissez-faire policy. It went beyond the school gate too. As Kath noted the school connected with students' home lives in order to ensure compliance:

> We've got letters or phone calls, you know, when we've got kids that don't look like they're going to meet the deadline or they can't show a draft, we'll ring home and say, hey listen, you know, what's happening at home, is there some issue that your student hasn't finished and they're in danger of failing this assignment, so what can we do to help.

These regulatory mechanisms are designed to know the students' home-life but only as a means to ensure that they fulfil the performative expectations of the school. Kath's vigilance regarding performance is associated with a theory of learning based on habit formation and a strong sense that students need to be supported in developing the habits of self-regulation. As she indicated:

> So, we try really hard about not letting kids slip through the net because it becomes a pattern with them, like truancy, you know, once they start doing it and then get some success from it they just keep doing it, and it's really hard to break that cycle.

Kath also accepted that it was the teachers' and the school's responsibility to act as the monitor of the students' habit formation at least until the senior years of schooling:

> (If) they're failing because they're not handing work in or it's late all the time well then that's just appalling, you know, and you can't say 'oh well, they're responsible', because in fact, like, until their senior (years) I don't think they're responsible, you know what I mean, (the seniors) can make those decisions for themselves. So, while it might be a bit punitive, probably, and I mean, and teachers are pretty good here, they'll work with kids, they'll stay back at morning tea and lunch and help them do it, and we encourage them to ring parents all the time.

The key phrase in the extract above–'and you can't say "oh well, they're responsible", because in fact, like, until their senior I don't think they're responsible'–is a remarkable statement about the philosophy and values of Kath regarding the behaviour of students. It was not that she blamed the students, nor did she see them in deficit terms as simply badly behaved young people. She saw it as the school's collective responsibility to ensure the students performed and achieved to their 'potential'. The strong emotional phrase about allowing students to fail–'well then that's just appalling'–conveys the strength of her conviction about the school's responsibility. She seems to be aware that this might seem tough to us as the interviewers–'So, while it might be a bit punitive', and she follows this with a statement about how much care and support the teachers offer–'they'll work with kids, they'll stay back at morning tea and lunch and help them do it'–as well vigilance and contact with the parents–'and we encourage them to ring parents all the time'. So the re-education and compliance practices at Red Point High require real investment of time and energy from teachers, and as noted above this is interpreted by students as 'harsh but caring'.

Cassandra, the school welfare officer at Red Point High (see extract below), also linked care to 'not letting them be slack'. She deployed a 'tough love' discourse that centred responsibility for good behaviour and commitment on students but scaffolded their shift from teacher-regulation to full self-regulation. That is, maintaining standards for this teacher was linked to her pedagogical task of building them up and teaching them organisational skills. In her rich commentary, she restated Kath's sense of outrage that students might fail not due to lack of capacity but simply by not getting organised and fulfilling the procedural requirements of schooling, such as submitting homework or assignments:

> My kids know that if their homework is not done, they either have to have a note from home, or they get a detention. Or they come and see me before class, you know, make an effort. I just don't lower my standards that way. Not letting them be slack. A lot of it is being disorganised; they just need organisational skills; teaching them how to be organised, building them up.
>
> (Cassandra)

The concern with preserving the school's reputation was found throughout the school. This did lead to teachers cajoling, harassing, encouraging and inspiring students to engage with the curriculum and to put effort into their work (see Ladson-Billing 1995). However, in many instances, demonstrating care for the students was not solely based upon maintaining the reputation of the school, but also the academic success of the individual student.

Throughout our teacher interviews we were given examples of how teachers cared for those students in particular who were perceived as struggling. Comments like the following were common in these interviews:

> I think [the school is] pretty supportive [of the culture of Indigenous kids]. I know if I have a student that can't read or write, I'll go and see the deputy straight away and say 'I'm willing to give up some classes to sit with this person, and get through assignments; do a little bit of reading on the side'. I'll always ask the student 'Are you comfortable if you sit with me and read? I'll get books that you'll be able to cope with'.
>
> (Larissa)

> I had one kid last year who never handed in an assessment, and it would always go missing. I would get so cranky. So I ended up ringing Dad . . . there was only Dad on the scene. He was pulling his hair out; he didn't know what was going on. I'll write in the diary when things are due, or I'll email you to let you know when things are due. That made a huge improvement, because Dad could then follow up.
>
> (Fiona)

We would suggest that such care is indicative of the ways in which teachers at the school took up the expectations inherent in the school's reputation. They are prepared to go out of their way and to invest time and effort to ensure that non-compliant students hand in their assignments, improve the quality of their work and learn new skills and knowledge. However, this care is still located within the frame of enhancing the academic work of students. We are not suggesting that this is unimportant. The efforts of these teachers may very well make a significant difference to the students with whom they are working. We are suggesting, however, that this is a limited notion of care, and one that fails to see the significance of education beyond a concern with academic outcomes.

To sum up, in this section of the chapter we have considered how care at Red Point High was tightly entwined with the politics of differentiation through: 1) policing entry to the school community and excluding those who might damage its reputation, and 2) regulating the behaviour and performance of the students within the community to ensure compliance and success as defined by the institution. Over many years and eras, involving different principals and teachers, Red Point High has manufactured the image of a school for academic students, as a place with high expectations, but also where students are cared for, especially in terms of inculcating practical habits and forms of self-regulation that ensure success. This imaginary community of successful students, as with all such constructs, is fragile and requires constant maintenance and policing. This is evident in the ways that teachers are constantly harassing, punishing, prompting and encouraging and supporting students' engagement in school tasks, with benefits for both the individual student and the reputation of the school. Such approaches to care, however, are anchored in a technical rationality that treats student disengagement as a deficit in self-regulation, as a lack of practical habits and organisational skills. Such deficits may even extend into the home, and Red Point High seeks contact with the home when non-compliance with school practices becomes serious. That the students interpret these disciplining mechanisms as caring for them would seem to indicate that the school has largely been successful in this disciplinary work. Also some of these marginal community members (non-compliant students) will eventually achieve similar success as the more compliant students and so this form of caring could be regarded as exemplifying distributive justice because effort and energy is expended by teachers to ensure widespread success. However, as with many others (see Fraser 2008; Keddie 2012; Mills 2001; Young 1990), we view social justice as extending beyond issues of redistribution. Valuing and recognising difference and enabling voices of dissent to be heard all relate to social justice. We have dealt with some of these issues in other chapters. Here we want to extend our discussions of 'differentiation' and care by going beyond distributive understandings of social justice to include a consideration of what Lynch has referred to as 'affective equality' (Lynch 2012). In so doing we recognise that care is central to the 'relational order' (Lynch et al. 2007, p.13) of the school that cannot be addressed simply by caring about behavioural compliance and academic achievement. Indeed, these latter performative discourses too often create contexts where concern with relational care for individuals and groups is stifled (Lynch et al. 2007).

Care and affective equality

Regardless of the performative culture within schools, the very relational nature of teaching leads to the development of 'caring' relationships between students and teachers. Interacting face to face on a daily basis inevitably creates shared moments of mutuality and empathy as well as episodes of conflict and strong emotions. The embodied nature of the daily interaction between teachers and students makes it very difficult for teachers not to care about individual students' emotional, spiritual and physical wellbeing. This can be a negative form of care as well as a positive form, for example, in cases where teachers want students excluded from their classes or the school for the benefit of others. In this section of the chapter we explore the relational aspects of care that emerged in our interviews with teachers and students, and we look for the gaps and spaces available within the school to pursue a social justice agenda framed around notions of affective equality. We explore also how an expanded understanding of 'differentiation' might be deployed to enhance this agenda.

Many teachers at Red Point High avoided political and social engagement with students and their community, as indicated in the previous section. However, some teachers at the school did engage and relate to students and their families in ways consistent with a politics of care that aligned with understandings of affective equality (Lynch et al. 2007). This politics was apparent in several key stories that we heard in interviews. These stories reflected the embodied and lived experience of teaching and learning where teachers focused on supporting particular students, connecting with their cultural resources, their challenges, their families and communities and their cultural and political positioning in society. They reflected teachers' deep interest in students and, as such, were acutely mindful of the complexities and specificities of the contexts within which teachers teach and students learn–complexities and specificities so often washed out of current neo-liberally framed and performative notions of what constitutes quality teachers and teaching. The constructions of care threading through these stories resonate with how care has been theorised in feminist work. Such work has drawn attention to the salience of care and love as goods of public significance and has highlighted the imperative of care as a human capability key to meeting a basic human need (see Nussbaum 2001). Such feminist constructions of care have had a major impact in the sphere of education (see Noddings 1988). In this work care and love as public goods are positioned in sharp contrast to the hyper-rationality and pragmatism endemic in the culture of western schooling. They also contrast with, but can complement, some of the practices of institutional care highlighted in the previous section.

Care and solidarity, as requisite to socially just schooling, require close attention to how teachers relate to students on a daily basis and their moral struggles in this close interactive space. In pursuing social justice, these relations are obviously complex and framed by particular value-laden interests and choices. In relation to redistributive, recognitive and representative justice, as Lynch (2010) argues, 'people are evaluative; they make moral judgements about what matters to them . . . their decisions are influenced by their love, care and solidarity priorities and values' (p.12). For Lynch (2010, p.3) affective equality is based on a number of key premises:

> First, that humans live in profound states of dependency and interdependency and are therefore relational beings; second, that people are deeply vulnerable at several levels, corporeally, emotionally, socially, politically,

> culturally and economically; and thirdly, that people are sentient beings, with relational identities and feelings (both positive and negative) and that these feelings and identities play an important role in informing normative rationality; relational feelings influence choices about what is good and bad, moral and immoral.

A politics of care framed by such premises moves beyond a positioning of disadvantaged or marginalised students along deficit lines where poor academic achievement is attributed to social or cultural lack. It is a pedagogy that moves beyond these low expectations and the degraded teaching that generally follows to a focus on the arrangements (both within and beyond the school) that must be in place in order to maximise the learning potential of disadvantaged students (see Keddie 2012; Gillborn & Ladson-Billings 2004; Mills & Gale 2010a; 2010b). It is a pedagogy of care that while not uncomplicated can cut through the rigidities and hyper-rationalities of school cultures that alienate and marginalise learners.

Below we explore a number of episodes of care reported by teachers at Red Point High that seem to cut through the rigidities and hyper-rationalities of neo-liberal schooling. Teachers expressed sensitivity and responsiveness to the various contextual factors inhibiting students' school participation and achievement, especially their home circumstances. For example, Charlie stated:

> There definitely have been times when I've thought, 'That kid is just so lazy; what a lazy, lazy kid!' and then you find out things about their family, their home, and then you think, 'That makes sense why you're not really focusing on work'. I've had times when I've had a kid that I've tried to give him this assignment, but he's falling asleep in class. And I've been trying to get through some work with him; then found out that at home his Mum is working ridiculous hours, and the Dad–the good relationship had gone; he's been having to look after kids. It's difficult.

For teachers like Charlie, care discourses centred upon understanding that 'the journey between home and school [for many students] influences the way they experience and contribute to their days [at] school' and that supporting better educational outcomes for disadvantaged students means supporting them to 'navigate successfully the distance between the world of home and school to facilitate a comfortable fit for all students in the school environment' (Dilg 2003, p.8).

In discussing this journey, teachers we interviewed at Red Point High commented on a distinct mismatch between the home culture of the disadvantaged students and the culture of the school. Certainly, these students' home cultures were positioned as not supportive in terms of school learning:

> The majority of the kids, their disadvantage comes from their homelife . . . we have a lot of students from separated families, and end up being in that disadvantaged category.
>
> (Charlie)

> A lot of the lower level kids, in terms of their work, they've got no one to feed them, never mind see their homework. Plenty of kids have no food. Those sorts of kids are quite itinerant. If you ask them, 'Why are you so tired?', 'I was up till 3 o'clock', 'I haven't had anything to eat'.
>
> (Pamela)

These comments might be read as subscribing to deficit understandings of students' home circumstances, for example, in associating a lack of appropriate care and disorganisation with parental and home circumstances in implicit binary opposition to the appropriate care and organisation of the school. Such deficit constructions are, of course, problematic. Notwithstanding these problematics, clearly apparent in the comments is the teachers' recognition of the reality that there are elements within students' backgrounds that compromise their educational performance. Teachers are trying to understand their students within the moral parameters of school participation and achievement. Recognising these parameters and mobilising one's own empathy and understanding are central to affective equality because they lead to analysis of the necessary economic, cultural and political support required to maximise learning for these students.

Importantly, certain teachers engaged in critical self-reflection in relation to this discourse of care. In particular, teachers reflected on their struggle over values and emotions in this space, as the following comments by Kath about her own childhood indicate:

> I think family life has a great impact. I know, myself, when growing up, my parents always made me do my homework. If it wasn't for that, I'm not sure that I would have done as well–if I didn't have that extra support and encouragement to see school as a high priority. If families don't see school as a high priority. . . . If no-one comes to pick them up, or help out in weather like this, they're the ones who pressure themselves to come to school. No-one comes to wake them up. They've got to do it themselves, and they've got to walk through the rain to get to school. I know, myself, if Mum said I had to walk through the rain to get to school, I wouldn't go!

Kath's discourse of care–her connections with her disadvantaged students–prompts her to think of her own position of privilege and its positive impacts on her school attendance. Reflecting on this position seems to foster a greater sense of connectedness to the difficulties confronting her students who do not 'have that extra support and encouragement to see school as a high priority'. Such reflection is key to differentiating care in relation to social justice and to pursuing affective equality. Central here are: 1) teachers understanding and locating marginalised students' ways of being within the context of their particular backgrounds, and 2) disrupting the norms that frame their invariably race and class privileged lives (Fraser 1997; Young 1990). From this 'de-centred' position, as is well recognised (see Davies 2000; Ellsworth 1989), educators can better see and transform the inequitable relations of power and authority that can disenfranchise students. Importantly, Kath's comment indicates not only the importance of connecting with and learning from students, but also that educators' views of students are partial, interested and potentially oppressive (see Ellsworth 1989).

For other teachers, a similar discourse of care from a moral position of sensitivity and responsiveness to students' personal lives was evident:

> I think that we recognise that they have personal lives, and sometimes those personal lives impinge on their learning, and somehow, some way, that has to be recognised because we have to get them to feel comfortable and safe and relaxed at school. . . .
>
> (Karen)

Along similar lines, developing caring relations for students required 'getting to know' students. As Kath indicated:

> I certainly do appreciate knowing a kid's full story because it does make a difference. And I certainly do believe that unless you have an emotional respect and bonding, you're not going to get those lower level ones to come up and put in a word.

However, it is not always that simple, as another teacher indicated:

> . . . if I know what's happening (at home), I can gauge how to help them with their assessment. They might need a bit of extra time, maybe . . . but you can't be too invasive; you've got to be very delicate about it.
>
> (Pamela)

Such 'delicacy' and 'not being too invasive' indicates that intruding into students' personal lives is not always welcome and may well damage the 'caring relationship' between students and teachers. Knowing 'too much' about the students may also work to prejudice teachers against students (for example, knowing that a student has been in trouble with juvenile justice outside of school). This was recognised by the Red Point High administration, as Pamela indicated:

> I think it's changed a bit this year, but this school is very very strict about knowing things on a need-to-know basis. No-one should know things that you don't have to know. . . . I think the idea is that we don't go in and treat kids in certain ways because we know things about them. This is the reverse of my old school, where they thought we should know things about the kids, so that we would treat them in a certain way. . . .

However, according to most of the teachers, responsiveness to the difficulties in students' home-lives was central to supporting them to feel 'comfortable', 'safe' and 'relaxed' at school so that they could achieve. While a 'delicate' process, such responsiveness works towards an affective equality. Pamela's statements in particular highlight the importance of care being a relational practice that is cognisant of student agency. Students will not always be prepared to divulge all personal information about themselves to teachers or may feel resentful at having had to divulge aspects of their lives that they would have liked to keep private. Respecting student autonomy along these lines was important in teachers' efforts to create relations of rapport and trust with students.

Several teachers elaborated on the importance of rapport and trust with students especially for disadvantaged students, contrasting themselves with other teachers at Red Point High who 'didn't care' or who were authoritarian:

> It's difficult for them (students), because the ones who do have so much going on in their lives outside of school, and then they've got teachers who don't seem to care about them. The kids feel that. They don't have that rapport with them. They just, they don't take the time to get to know them, and don't try to support them. Even if it's just saying 'How are you going today?'
>
> (Karen)

Another teacher stressed the importance of being responsive to events or moods that were shaping students' behaviours at any given time:

> I had one student last year–he had a few anger issues, another Indigenous student. There were times when I knew he was angry. I said 'I don't mind if you do nothing. Just go and get a drink, and come back. We can talk about it later if you want to; if not, that's fine'. Some teachers may not respond in that way; they'd say 'Get your book out. Let's get started'.
>
> (Lenore)

These instances of affective sensitivity and adjustment by teachers suggest an expanded and enriched notion of differentiation that goes beyond concerns with the technicalities of curriculum pedagogy and assessment to concerns about relating to particular students with empathy and understanding. For example, one teacher described how she had worked hard over the year to engage a struggling student who eventually achieved a B grade in English. This was a significant improvement and so the teacher contacted his mother to share the good news.

Importantly, the teacher did not share the grade with the mother simply as an assessment outcome. Rather the grade signified that the student/son had become a different person, or as the teacher reported to us, 'I wanted the mother to see the person that I see in him'. The teacher's caring work is about the student's identity and her effort to reveal new possibilities for his life through concrete achievements at school. Her work had enabled him to experience a new self, one who is capable of learning and succeeding. This work of caring is about ontology, about who these students could become rather than who they currently are within their social networks.

There were other care stories that we heard from teachers that highlighted the emotional, relational and time-consuming work of teachers' personal investment in creating new educational identities for students. One was a heart-wrenching story of a girl whose brother took his own life. As his own short life was spiralling down, she had promised him she would try to do better at school, and after his death she achieved a whole term without receiving a 'blue slip'. The Indigenous liaison worker at Red Point High exclaimed, 'Man alive, you've had no blue slips!'. This juxtaposition of tragedy in the lives of Indigenous youth and striving to do well at school sets the mundane events of the classroom in a significant light. Surviving at school and in life are measured in small daily victories of avoiding blue slips and getting assignments completed. How do caring teachers manage these incidental events in school life? Some teachers note that they bend and apply school rules flexibly at times to give certain students space and time to calm down and manage their emotions. Aileen also provides a physical space (her designated room with comfortable chairs and snack food) where Indigenous students can come to share their worries, tell her about negative occurrences with other students or teachers and celebrate their victories. It is in these everyday passing moments that teachers can support students and create opportunities for them to re-imagine themselves at school as successful and engaged. The techniques of establishing expectations are not simply technical activities but occur at the intersection of care, emotions and relationships.

These stories illustrate the educational significance of care labour. It is not a given that teachers in schools will care about students in ways that will enable them to flourish academically and socially. As Lynch et al. (2007, p.13) argue:

> There is nothing inevitable in the love, care and solidarity world; the relational sphere provides contexts when it can happen but also a context where it can be destroyed. Being-with-others is a condition of human existence . . . what care, love and solidarity relations have in common is that they all involve relations of dependence and interdependence, relations of giving and receiving, and relations of power. They are all part of the relational order.

The affective engagement of teachers in the accounts above indicates their efforts to enable relational care. In so doing they acknowledge the significance of students' backgrounds and home-lives in shaping their experiences of schooling and the potential disjunctures between school and home; and they recognise and set aside their own privilege in such acknowledgement. A critical aspect of this care is also the forging of relations based upon rapport and trust, which encourages students to heed their advice, their encouragement and even their admonishments. Rapport and trust also entail not pushing students to divulge information that they consider too private to reveal; it involves respecting student autonomy. At times it also means being flexible in relation to school rules and expectations and responsive in terms of students' immediate needs. Differentiating care along these lines is a key imperative for creating socially just schooling. Underpinning many of the accounts was a concern with who gets care. Whilst perhaps using deficit constructions of some young people's families, teachers were seeking to ensure that certain young people did not miss out on care. Important here is recognising that not everybody has the same access to emotional, as well as material and human resources. A socially just differentiation of care would recognise the importance of ensuring that those who have missed out on care outside of school receive it in school. However, it would also entail a recognition of the oppressions and injustices at a broader structural or institutionalised level that contribute to the affective inequality that students might experience at a personal level. This brings us to solidarity.

Solidarity and affective equality

Alongside the care stories were also stories of solidarity. At the time of our first visit to the school the boundary work that had been undertaken to ensure that the school community retained its academic reputation and identity was put under threat by the appointment of a new principal. Phil, like his predecessors, was also concerned with the reputation of the school and wanted to maintain its high academic standards and was, as indicated in Chapter 2, very concerned with the quality of the pedagogy and curriculum being experienced by students. However, he also brought a more inclusive agenda to the school. This was most evident in his commitment to social justice in relation to Indigenous issues, such as including an Acknowledgement of Country at the school assembly (see Chapter 1). Like the flagpole initiative that we described in the introduction to this book, the practice of Acknowledgement of Country exemplifies solidarity work towards affective equality. Representing marginalised groups along these lines of group identity is important, as we have mentioned earlier, as a political strategy for institutional and social change (hooks 2003). The way in which 'acknowledgements of country' now occur at multiple formal events in Australia (for example the opening of parliaments, university graduations and major academic conferences) is indicative of the way in which the landscape has changed in Australian political and social life in terms of a more inclusive society. However, it is well recognised that these sort of initiatives can be taken up in tokenistic ways that reproduce inequities (Benhabib 2002; Fraser 2008; Gay 2000, see also Chapter 6 for elaboration).

It may well be that the changing nature of the context at Red Point High, stimulated through some of Phil's actions, generated an inclusive environment. While there was resistance to Indigenous inclusion at the school, as we have already detailed, there were also aspects that countered this resistance. For example, for the first time three of the five key student leadership positions at the school were occupied by Indigenous students. These were elected positions open to all senior students at the school. Phil told us:

> The Indigenous community here seems to have welcomed me pretty well and that may well have been why more kids have come here, because some families have been prepared to . . . I mean, a lot of it to me is, you know, you

> just gotta not be quite so stuck up about the way things are done and, you know, the Indigenous culture is a very rich and important part of schooling here and, you know, I'm wrapped to see, you know, that there's three Indigenous leaders who were elected into those positions, not in a tokenistic way but on their merits, you know, along with the white Anglo-Saxon population.

That there were some within the school who were uncomfortable with these changes was understood by Phil in the following ways:

> I mean there's a rich, deep, history in the culture of the school with certain people that have been here a very long time and with all respect to them they give their heart and soul to the place and they work very hard. In some cases, it's a case of if you don't know what you don't know and I think you know, so it's probably it's a little bit challenging for some people . . . what I hope is that, in the long term, people see that, overall, it is better for the school. You know, I'm really hoping that people are open-minded enough to see that as time goes by, you know, it hasn't, you know, turned it into an Indigenous ghetto or, you know, like, that it's been detrimental. That in fact that more kids are coming and they're achieving well and, you know, that's my hope.

The issues and concerns raised in this section exemplify the 'tertiary relations' of care highlighted by Lynch et al. (2007), where solidarity work is less individual and personal–that is, such work tends to be concerned with broader groups to whom we feel care responsibilities through moral or statutory obligations. What is important here is that efforts at Red Point High are focused on creating the context and conditions to support social action and to express solidarity. This is key to pursuing social justice in relation to (in particular) political representation (see Fraser 2008) and was important at Red Point High in relation to attempting to remedy the marginalisation of Indigenous students and their community. Pursuing affective equality along these lines is, of course, highly significant work, and can have significant costs to the moral agents of change. As we detail in Chapter 6, the group identity politics that such solidarity work engages with are not unproblematic. While a group identity politic is very useful in working towards political (representative) justice where all are accorded a voice in decision-making (see hooks 2003), it can differentiate in ways that undermine social justice through essentialising and reifying difference as other and deficit (Fraser 2008). In this particular case the selection of Indigenous students as leaders by the whole school population is a positive sign that othering has been minimised and that the recognition by the students themselves of Indigenous identity and culture within the school has been accepted as part of the emerging culture at Red Point High under the leadership of Phil. In this respect the students seem to be more attuned to recognitive justice than some of the teachers who resisted Phil's acknowledgement of country and procurement of the extra flagpole.

Conclusion

A key feature of differentiated classrooms, differentiated assessment and differentiated curricula is the supposed provision of opportunities for some students who have experienced very little academic success to improve their academic outcomes. In order to do this we have argued that schools and teachers need to care about their students. This was evident in the previous chapter on high expectations. However, and we are of the view that Red Point High is not alone in this, the care that is performed by policies and practices within the school prioritise a care for the institution of the school and its reputation. There are benefits to this in that reputations based on high expectations and high academic achievement, when accompanied by support programs for those students from marginalised backgrounds who are struggling with schoolwork, can improve the life chances of many students.

The stories of care told by administrators, teachers and students at Red Point High represented concerns for both institutional care and investments by teachers in the relational order of the school. Thus we heard stories of distant institutional care that involved students coming to see that Red Point High cared for them by maintaining high standards for their behaviour, by chasing up on them when they did not do their work and by teachers wanting them to succeed. In most instances this institutional care was low in emotional investment from the teachers. The focus was on students transitioning from disruptive behaviour, where they experience the behaviour management protocols of Red Point High including suspensions, to willing acceptance of the management of their behaviour and acceptance of the Red Point High culture.

However, we also heard stories of personal investment by teachers in co-creating new identities for the students and mediating new relationships between the students, the school and their parents. In these stories the teachers acted 'as if' the students were capable of learning and achieving more than their previous history would predict. The 'as if' stance of the teachers opens up a space for students to re-imagine themselves as more capable.

We also heard stories of solidarity. These stories of care were concerned with different populations and were not usually related to individual students. Of significance within the school was the care demonstrated towards Indigenous groups and to ensuring that students from such backgrounds were not marginalised within the school *and* that Indigenous cultures and knowledges were valued by the school's non-Indigenous population. Here Phil was seeking to ensure that care for the reputation of the school did not undermine a socially just approach to the wellbeing of Indigenous students and the local community.

Engaging with the politics of differentiation in schools requires a consideration of how differential treatment for different students or groups of students can enhance socially just outcomes from schooling, both academic and social. In this chapter we have argued that care and solidarity are important ingredients in this consideration. Care about the school and about the rules, regulations and expectations is often primary within the relational order of schools. However, the personal investment that comes from caring about different students is always going to be based on the uniqueness of an interaction between two people. What the teachers at Red Point High demonstrated is that the investment needs to be greater for those who are struggling with school, with their out-of-school lives or particular life events.

Considerations of differentiation also require a consideration of different groups and the ways in which they experience injustice. At Red Point High, the focus has been on Indigenous groups; such a focus could just as easily be in relation to other racial or ethnic minorities, LGBTI students or girls. In such cases there are broader concerns about social justice and difference that are not necessarily related to individual students. For many teachers, and in many schools, unless that marginalised group is obviously present, little effort goes into challenging such injustices. One teacher told us:

> Quite often I get the impression that we don't think about [diverse kids] as much as we should. It's very easy to look at this school and say, 'They all look like they come from the same . . .' It's very easy to go in and pretend that they all are this.
>
> (Charlie)

The professional work of caring challenges such homogenising of difference by prioritising the relational and personal in teaching. As we have shown in this chapter, the personal is political in the work of care because it requires allocating time, resources and affective energy to relate to students, and challenges regimes in school that seek simply technical and efficient solutions to education goals.

In the following chapter we investigate how Crimson High pursued a social justice agenda through its curriculum. We highlight the complexity of ensuring that a diverse set of curriculum pathways designed to cater to the perceived needs and interests of 'all' students does not become a corridor to nowhere for the more marginalised students at the school. However, we also note how this differentiation can act in some instances as a 'hook' to engage such students, broaden their opportunities and open up life pathways for them.

References

Bauman, Z 2001, *Community: Seeking safety in an insecure world*, Polity Press, Cambridge.

Benhabib, S 2002, *The claims of culture: Equality and diversity in the global era*, Princeton University Press, New Jersey.

Blackmore, J 1999, *Troubling women: Feminism, leadership and educational change*, Open University Press, Buckingham.

Blackmore, J 2006, 'Social justice and the study and practice of leadership in education: A feminist history', *Journal of Educational Administration and History*, Vol. 38, no. 2, pp. 185–200.

Boler, M 1999, *Feeling power: Emotions and education*, Routledge, New York.

Davies, B 2000, *A body of writing, 1990–1999*. AltaMira Press, Walnut Creek.

Dilg, M (ed) 2003, *Thriving in the multicultural classroom: Principles and practices for effective teaching*. Teachers' College Press, New York.

Ellsworth, E 1989, 'Why doesn't this feel empowering? Working through the repressive myths of critical pedagogy', *Harvard Educational Review*, Vol. 59, no. 3, pp. 297–325.

Fraser, N 1997, *Justice interruptus: Critical reflections on the 'postsocialist' condition*, Routledge, New York.

Fraser, N 2008, 'Rethinking recognition: Overcoming displacement and reification in cultural politics', In *Adding insult to injury: Nancy Fraser debates her critics*, ed K Olson, Verso, London, pp. 129–141.

Gay, G 2000, *Culturally responsive teaching: Theory, research, and practice*, Teacher's College Press, New York.

Gillborn, D & Ladson-Billings, G 2004, *The Routledge Falmer reader in multicultural education*, Routledge, New York.

Hochschild, AR 1983, *The managed heart: The commercialization of human feeling*. University of California Press, Berkeley.

hooks, b 2003, *Teaching community: A pedagogy of hope*, Routledge, New York.

Keddie, A 2012, *Educating for diversity and social justice*, Routledge, New York.

Keddie, A, Mills, M, & Pendergast, D 2011, 'Fabricating an identity in neo-liberal times: Performing schooling as "number one"', *Oxford Review of Education*, Vol. 37, no. 1, pp. 75–92.Ladson-Billings, G 1995, 'Toward a theory of culturally relevant pedagogy', *American Educational Research Journal*, Vol. 32, no. 3, pp. 465–491.

Lynch, K 2010, 'Affective equality: Love, care and solidarity as productive forces', In *Proceedings from GEXcel. CFS Report Series; No. 14; Tema Genus Report Series, No.12*. ed Sofia Strid and Anna G Jónasdóttir. Available from: http://research repository.ucd.ie. [13 November 2013].

Lynch, K 2012, 'Affective equality as a key issue of justice: A comment on Fraser's 3-dimensional framework', *Social Justice Series*, Vol. 12, no. 3, pp. 45–64.

Lynch, K, Lyons, M, & Cantillon, S 2007, 'Breaking silence: Educating citizens for love, care and solidarity', *International Studies in Sociology of Education*, Vol. 17, no. 1–2, pp. 1–19.Maguire, M, Perryman, J, Ball, S, & Braun, A 2011, 'The ordinary school–What is it?', *British Journal of Sociology of Education*, Vol. 32, no. 1, pp. 1–16.

Masters, G 2009, *A shared challenge: Improving literacy, numeracy and science learning in Queensland primary schools*, Australian Council for Educational Research, Melbourne.

Mills, C & Gale, T 2010a, 'Coming to terms with social inequalities in education', *Schooling in Disadvantaged Communities*, Springer, Netherlands, pp. 13–27.

Mills, C & Gale, T 2010b, 'Acquiring a feel for the game', *Schooling in Disadvantaged Communities* Springer, Netherlands, pp. 89–103.

Mills, M 2001, *Challenging violence in schools: An issue of masculinities*, Open University Press, Buckingham.

Mills, M, Renshaw, P, & Zipin, L 2013, 'Alternative education provision: A dumping ground for "wasted lives" or a challenge to the mainstream?', *Social Alternatives*, Vol. 32, no. 2, pp. 13–18.

Noddings, N 1988, 'An ethic of caring and its implications for instructional arrangements', *American Journal of Education*, Vol. 96, no. 2, pp. 215–230.

Nussbaum, M 2001, *Upheavals of thought: The intelligence of emotions*, Cambridge University Press, Cambridge.

Sarra, C 2003, Cherbourg State School: Strong and smart. *What Works Program: Improving Outcomes for Indigenous Students.* Available from: http://www.whatworks.edu.au. [1 July 2012].

Sarra, C 2008, *School accountability: Asking some overdue hard questions*, Indigenous Education Leadership Institute, Caboolture, Qld.

Young, I 1990, *Justice and the politics of difference*, Princeton University Press, New Jersey.

5 A politics of differentiation and curriculum

> My world has changed, and so has yours . . . it is our responsibility in schools to . . . create opportunities for students so they can take their place confidently and successfully as responsible citizens in an increasingly globalised world. . . . In an internationally minded, inclusive community differences of culture, gender, physical abilities, thinking style, profession, religion, family circumstances and generation are valued. . . . We are a world class school and a school that cares about the world.
>
> (Geoff)

Geoff, the principal of Crimson High, had been in the role for decades, and he articulated a strong commitment to social justice. For him, being a socially just school meant that the school catered to the needs of all of its students and that it encouraged students to become active citizens in a changing world. The social justice principles of recognition and representation were important to him. As the quote above indicates, Geoff wanted the school to be a place where differences of all kinds were valued and recognised. He sought to ensure that the voices of those marginalised by difference were heard throughout the school via a variety of educational support programs. He was also concerned about issues of redistribution and poverty and wanted to ensure that students were not prevented from attending school.

However, as with the politics raised in other chapters, ongoing tensions affected Crimson High, particularly with regard to redistribution. Their approach to curriculum attempted to hook students into the process of schooling by offering a wide range of curriculum options and pathways, yet these inevitably remained differentiated by status and transferable worth at graduation. Data for Crimson High available from the MySchool website indicates that about 30 per cent of graduating students proceeded to university study. Another 20 per cent entered further education at Technical and Further Education (TAFE) colleges, while about 30 per cent entered directly into employment opportunities. This leaves a sizeable proportion (20 per cent) of graduates from Crimson High who appeared to be neither 'learning nor earning'. The leadership at Crimson High did not ignore the challenge of trying to ensure that each graduate had opportunities for relevant further study and employment. But clearly the challenge remains for Crimson High and all schools to ensure there is 'curricular justice' (Connell 1993), that is, ensuring that curriculum options and pathways do not become corridors to nowhere. This is the tension that we explore in this chapter, acknowledging at the outset that Crimson High is well aware of the challenges of ensuring curricular justice. Clearly, there are no scripted easy answers, but we can offer some insights into possible ways forward by interrogating the practices we were able to document and observe at Crimson.

Our aim during our many visits to Crimson High was to investigate how the school was engaging students who were otherwise struggling to achieve academic success. Central to this we wanted to know what flexibility existed in the curriculum, whether through the formal or informal curriculum, that would enable students to draw on their own experiences, or funds of knowledge, to enhance their learning at school (Gonzalez, Moll & Amanti 2005; Zipin, Sellar & Hattam 2012). Through our interviews with teachers and students we wanted to open up conversations about learning and the impact of the school's extensive curriculum offerings on students' lives. Underpinning our conversations were the following questions: Does a wide and diverse range of curriculum offerings support or hinder social justice (Collins & Yates 2011)? Who is accessing 'powerful knowledges' and who misses out when student 'choice' underpins curriculum selections (Young 2011)? Can extra- and co-curricular offerings provide hooks into formal academic curricula? And indeed, as the comment from the principal, Geoff, of Crimson High indicates above: What are schools for (MacAllister 2016)?

Crimson High had put substantial effort into providing a wide range of opportunities for its students by offering a broad and very differentiated curriculum (with over 60 academic and vocational–Vocational Education and Training (VET)–subjects), support programs and career pathways. It offers an Academic Excellence program as well as specialist programs in sports, music and dance. The school's commitment to supporting all students was further enhanced when the school underwent an evaluation process leading to accreditation by the Council of International Schools. These attempts can be read as supporting social justice in their recognition and valuing of, and connecting with, the diversity of interests and preferences that students at Crimson brought to school. Geoff was strongly committed to social justice and, as indicated above, was an advocate for those young people marginalised by poverty and difference:

> The world is not a level playing field. Some kids have it tougher. It's discriminatory to treat them all the same, because they're not all the same.

This highly differentiated curriculum could, however, be read as inhibiting social justice aims. Often differentiating the curriculum is a *de facto* way of streaming and setting classes. Curriculum hierarchies make sure of that.

In this chapter we draw on the voices of Geoff and 'Wendy' (Deputy Principal), 'Debra' (Youth Health Nurse), 'Lisa' and 'Julie' (teachers) and 'Ellie' (ancillary staff member) as well as students 'Jack', 'Tina' and 'Liam'. We consider some of the tensions which are brought about by attempting to provide a curriculum for all, such as the tensions between hierarchies of knowledges and vocational versus academic pathways. We ask: Does providing such a curriculum which is based on notions of difference (recognition) and taking into account student interests (representation) work to reproduce existing pathways based on socio-economic status, race and gender? Within this school there was a highly academic stream, and the school was understandably very proud of its students' academic successes. However, in its attempts to be a 'school for all' there were multiple non-academic pathways for students. This meant that there were many students, largely those from low socio-economic and marginalised cultural backgrounds, in those non-academic pathways who were missing out on what Young (2013) has referred to as 'powerful knowledge'. For Young:

> 'Powerful knowledge' is powerful because it provides the best understanding of the natural and social worlds that we have and helps us go beyond our individual experiences; even the creative and performing arts, and literature and drama, have these emergent properties and universalising properties, albeit not based on generalisations. Access to powerful knowledge in its diverse forms is an entitlement for all pupils and students. That is why the extent to which a curriculum is underpinned by 'powerful knowledge' is both an epistemological and a social justice issue.
>
> (2013, p.196)

He argues elsewhere that schools are the places where young people who have limited access to such knowledges in their everyday life can be exposed to them. He goes on to say: 'Thus on the grounds of popular relevance or pupil interest, the opportunities that students have for acquiring systematic theoretical knowledge that cannot be acquired elsewhere are restricted' (Young 2009, p.201). There were times then when we were of the view that the many curriculum pathways that were on offer for students actually represented 'corridors to nowhere'. By this we mean that they may not lead students to accessing the powerful knowledges to which Young refers, and thus, they may simply reinscribe and reproduce the broader inequities of the social world. That is to say, the diversity of curricular pathways at Crimson, while representing recognitive justice, may work to cement pathways of maldistribution it is these maldistributive pathways that we construe as 'corridors to nowhere'. At the same time we also acknowledge and problematise the notion of 'nowhere' in this view of curricular pathways given our broad view of the purposes of schooling (as needing to equally reflect both private [social mobility and credentialing] and public [democratic and social learning] goals), as we have argued elsewhere in this book.

However, it was also apparent to us that the many programs and curriculum streams within the school that appeared to lack the presence of such 'powerful knowledges' were the reason that students came to school. This brought tension into our views about the 'corridors to nowhere' notion, as these 'curriculum hooks' ensured that many young people attended school (the attendance data for Indigenous students was high compared to 'like schools' and was improving from year to year). In some cases these curriculum hooks facilitated students' engagement with the academic curriculum. Thus, in this chapter, by way of example, we discuss the school's music program as one such hook. Music is a curriculum area that is often not seen as providing utilitarian value, but which is extremely differentiated within the formal music curriculum catering to high academic performers and acting as a transmitter of high cultural capital via its repertoire of classical music, and the skills that are developed such as technical proficiency, group work and self-discipline (Wong 2005). However, it also has non-academic strands and is often introduced as an extracurricular activity that works to engage young marginalised people in schooling (Cleaver & Riddle 2014; McGregor & Mills 2006). We begin with a discussion of what constitutes curriculum.

What constitutes curriculum?

> As soon as you see him sleeping, summon all your might and main and hold him fast, although he strive and struggle to escape. He will make trial of you, turning into whatsoever moves on earth, to water even, and heaven-kindled fire; yet hold unflinchingly and clasp the more. . . .
>
> (*The Odyssey of Homer*, pp. 7–59)

In Homer's epic tales of extraordinary journeys, we encounter Menelaus, who will only be granted the information he needs to find his way home if he can hold on to Proteus, the old man of the sea, who constantly changes his physical form to avoid revealing his secrets. Not unlike Menelaus's challenge, the various constructs of curriculum appear slippery and impossible to pin down. This slipperiness is due in part to competing ideas about the role that curriculum plays in schooling. Several tensions emerge in attempting to respond to this challenge.

The curriculum is often perceived to be the set of formal documents that prescribe the teaching of particular knowledges and skills. What is to be included in these documents is often fiercely contested (Atweh & Singh 2011; Brennan 2011). In the Australian context this contestation has occurred with an increasingly centralised, federalised education system that has included the rollout of a national curriculum, the public reporting on student results in literacy and numeracy tests (via the MySchool website) and the implementation of literacy and numeracy testing for pre-service teachers. At the same time, there has been an increasing move to privatisation and corporatisation (Blum & Ullman 2012) through increasingly packaged educational products, including scripted lessons (MacDonald et al. 2008), and what Hogan et al. (2015) describe as 'edu-business'. There has also been a strengthening of subject hierarchies with a major focus on STEM (Science, Technology, Engineering and Mathematics), examples of 'powerful knowledge' or differentiated, specialised knowledges (Young & Muller 2013) that signify valued capital in today's curriculum.[1] Together these changes have contributed to a more highly regulated teaching environment, undermining teachers' professionalism and autonomy and leaving little time to make nuanced judgements about the needs of their students or plan their teaching and learning activities accordingly (Hyslop-Margison & Sears, 2010).

It has been argued from a social justice perspective that this situation works against marginalised students who are disadvantaged by rigid constructs of curriculum. For example, Woods et al. (2014) highlighted significant improvements in student learning when teachers and students worked together using collaborative planning and teaching and a 'distributed leadership' approach. Examples such as these challenge framings of curriculum as a unidirectional set of content descriptions and achievement standards that emanate from places where no young student sets foot. Instead, we are drawn to an interrogation of how knowledge is constructed and valued through the enactment of curriculum at the school level. We therefore ask: Is curriculum about knowledge construction or knowledge reconstruction? Whose knowledges are recognised through the curriculum? Whose knowledges are valued and how does the curriculum provide a space for marginalised and emerging constructs of knowledge? These questions primarily raise issues of recognition and representation.

However, it could be claimed that we know what knowledges are valued and what knowledges enable young people to productively engage with (and change) the world. Some would argue, and from a social justice perspective, as we indicated earlier, that currently only the most privileged students are being given access to these 'powerful knowledges' (Young 2011). This situation, in Fraser's terms, is an issue of maldistribution. The solution here, then becomes not differentiating the curriculum so that some, usually the most marginalised, miss out on these powerful knowledges, but actually narrowing the curriculum and limiting choice by specifying the importance of disciplinary knowledges for all. Some young, usually marginalised, people do not know what they are missing out upon by only making curriculum choices based on what 'interests' them. The latter, Young (2011) contends, is central to the emancipatory role of schools. He states:

> (Schooling) is also a unique opportunity for students to acquire–through subjects and their link to discipline-based knowledge–the knowledge that they would not have access to at home or at work.
>
> (2011, p.135)

It is such knowledge, which is often not in the homes or workplace of the most marginalised, which has the power to change society. This emancipatory role of schooling is, however, not often at the forefront of those developing curricula for schools.

Instead, schools are regularly seen as places where a society's human capital can be developed and where some, but not all, need powerful knowledges. This has meant that schools are often positioned as needing to respond quickly to social changes and the increasing complexity of the contemporary world, such as the effects of globalisation, changes in the work force needs of a society and new technologies (Young and Muller 2010). The opening quote of this chapter demonstrates one view of how schools should meet this challenge, by preparing its students to become confident, culturally inclusive citizens who care about the world. However, other views characterise schools as organisations that struggle to keep up with progress, progress being something that happens beyond the school gates. This type of framing often underlines a push to make curriculum more responsive to the needs of industry; some would argue that the way in which STEM subjects are currently being prioritised is an example of this (Tranter 2012). Tranter's discussion of this school–industry link harks back to well-worn debates about the 'sorting and selecting' function of schools (Apple 1979, p.43) and the ways that they reinforce class divisions. A key argument here has been for the need to democratise the curriculum in order to undermine these functions (Giroux 2010).

Lund and Carr (2008) argue that democracy needs to be 'infused' in all aspects of schooling, including curriculum. In this linking of schooling to democratic practices there is an opportunity to broaden the concept of curriculum beyond the formal prescriptive content and skills framing. Terwel (2005) argues that curriculum theory should be about educational planning which prioritises the development of the student. What this means in terms of how knowledges are constructed and defined is a current and politically charged debate. However, democratisation would suggest the creation of a curriculum which can cater to the perceived interests and abilities of all, typifying the concerns of those such as Rata (2012, p.xii) about the shift from 'academic knowledge' to 'the forces of localisation' in an attempt to make the curriculum more relevant to young learners. However, it is not just policy makers and curriculum designers who make decisions about the knowledge and skills that constitute the curriculum. At a school level, teachers and students make decisions about the relevance of the curriculum to their lives (Woods et al. 2014). Our inclusion of students' voices later in this chapter is an attempt to understand their experiences of a differentiated curriculum, adding to our collective interrogation of curriculum as it is enacted.

Notions of 'enacted curriculum' stand in contrast to definitions of curriculum, such as that of the Australian Curriculum, Assessment and Reporting Authority (ACARA), Australia's peak body for determining the school curriculum, which defines the curriculum as a set of formal documents to prescribe the teaching of knowledge and skills.[2] An enacted curriculum is clearly more than formal documents. Such a definition of curriculum renders invisible the myriad programs that complement and support 'formal' curriculum subjects and, in the case of Crimson High, programs that are intrinsic to ensuring students experience success with formal curriculum subjects. Together, these formal and informal subjects, support programs and extracurricular activities constitute the enacted curriculum, a practice which is 'brought to life in classrooms in relation to teachers' pedagogical content knowledge and students' cultural scripts and background schemata' (Luke 2010, p.2).

A differentiated curriculum in support of a social justice agenda

Curriculum differentiation has usually taken the form of either different curriculum pathways towards different post-school trajectories or separating students into 'ability groups' for all classes (streaming) or for individual subjects (setting) where 'harder' and 'easier' versions of the curriculum are tackled. Despite its common practice in UK and Australian schools, these approaches have attracted criticism for their tendency to further cement low achievement amongst students who already experience poor outcomes (Ireson et al. 2005; Sorhagen 2013; Terwel 2005). Moreover, Dunne et al. (2007) have commented that teachers' decisions about student placement into ability groups are often based on either shaky perceptions of a student's ability or on prior achievements, effectively lowering teacher expectations and students' motivation and self-esteem (see Chapter 3). In this section we consider how curriculum differentiation was implemented at Crimson High.

It is fair to say that we were very impressed talking to the leadership team at Crimson, that is, Geoff and Wendy, the deputy. They had been committed to the school for many years and saw themselves as providing a school that was inclusive of everyone from the community. They hoped that their work at Crimson High was slowly transforming the community and opening opportunities for a better life for the graduates from the school and their families. They were critically reflective professionals who worked tirelessly to offer real opportunities for the students to succeed. We regularly commented on the energy expended by Wendy, who not only maintained a broad set of administrative duties across the whole school, but also engaged with students between classes, in the playground and in the hallways, chatting to them and making sure they were on time and on task. It was impressive to observe over the weeks we collected data at Crimson High, but it was incredibly impressive to consider that this level of commitment had been maintained over decades.

The hallways and entry vestibule to the school were literally covered in photos celebrating students' achievements and awards in sports, in music, in academic excellence, in citizenship and in vocational and technical education. The sheer abundance of photographic evidence of diverse achievements conveyed the message that there was a place for everyone at the school. The community around Crimson High is quite disadvantaged and students enter into the first year of high school with widely divergent scores on basic literacy and numeracy. So the challenge was daunting in terms of offering a curriculum for everyone. Some students were already well along the way to excelling in the academic curriculum. Some students could not read. Some students had not missed a day of school in their lives. Some students had attended intermittently for their entire schooling careers. The notion of 'hooks' was coined by us to capture one of the ways that Crimson engaged with the diversity of students. A hook was a curriculum offering that might make school attractive and rewarding. Whether through offering a range of sports for boys and girls, or a range of music options, or informal curriculum options or targeted programs for groups of students, Crimson High seemed determined to engage students actively in learning.

During one of our early visits to Crimson High we used the phrase 'a school for all' as an attempt to capture the essence of our conversation with the school principal. The school's leadership team was acutely aware of the challenges it faced due to the low socio-economic backgrounds of many of the young people, and the phrase seemed to encapsulate the school's commitment to providing educational opportunities and a curriculum relevant to *all* its students. This commitment was framed as a focus on social justice. Wendy explained:

> I am committed here. And I guess part of it is, I have a very strong commitment . . . I think it's more that I do have a strong sense of social justice.

Being in a region identified by census data as having one of the highest rates of unemployment in Australia, the staff at Crimson High were conscious of the effects of poverty and how these manifested in the lives of their students:

> Quite a number of parents say 'We haven't sent our kids to school because they can't afford a pair of shoes, or they can't afford the uniform'. Some of them say 'We haven't got any food to give them'. . . . I was talking to a boy here the other day . . . [he asked] could he have an extension [on his assignment]. . . . He pays his Mum and Dad $100 a week board. I said 'Where do you get $100 from?' He said 'I work on the weekend' . . . we have kids who work, and they work every day of the week after school.
>
> (Geoff)

MySchool data for Crimson High indicate that academic achievement in national tests (in reading, writing, spelling, grammar, punctuation and numeracy) remains a challenge for the school, particularly amongst Indigenous students who make up approximately one-fifth of the student enrolments. Moreover as we indicated at the beginning of this chapter, further data show that in post-school destinations approximately one-third of senior secondary students continue to university study, whilst almost half move into vocational education study or take up employment. This contrasts with the overall numbers for the State of transitions to university that are approximately 7–8 per cent higher, although in relation to VET study this was almost equivalent.[3]

Participation in the curriculum offerings of any school is mediated concretely by students actually being at school, but regular attendance cannot be taken for granted in communities confronting poverty and social dislocation. At Crimson High, attendance data collected across a number of years had indicated that Indigenous and non-Indigenous participation at school differed markedly, with the rates for Indigenous students around 80 per cent and those of non-Indigenous students around 90 per cent. The response of the leadership at Crimson was to initiate personal contact with the families of each of the Indigenous students. This was a significant investment of resources in addressing curriculum access, as there were hundreds of families to visit. The Indigenous Liaison teachers and a group of assigned staff visited each family to talk about the student and the school, and seek ways to enhance their regular attendance. In these conversations the interests and aspirations of students were raised and connections with the curriculum offerings of the school were considered. This personal approach to addressing attendance was complemented by ongoing monitoring and accountability pressures maintained at school, where students were consistently asked to explain absences. The most recent attendance data indicated a clear shift in Indigenous participation, so it now is equivalent to that of non-Indigenous students. This set of practices is redistributive in that it addresses a material difference in access to the curriculum per se. The approach taken also indicates Crimson High's investment in community oriented solutions to what might otherwise by regarded as 'beyond the school gate' and the responsibility of parents. Crimson saw itself as responsible to draw students into the curriculum, and this entailed looking over the fence and seeking partnerships and connections.

Another way that the school has enacted its social justice agenda has been to build partnerships with the broader community, particularly with local industries. Their formal curriculum offers clearly defined programs to transition students from school to work or further study. Developing partnerships with business and industry is embedded in their curriculum planning and Vocational Education and Training programs, and is an attempt to ensure employment opportunities via apprenticeships and traineeships with local and regional businesses. These partnerships are highlighted regularly in their school newsletters and at public events. Conceptualising the curriculum in this way points to a larger discussion that is expanded upon in the next section in regard to the purpose of school in preparing its students for their lives post-school. Differentiated programs that are geared towards immediate employment opportunities can be seen as an important part of the curriculum to address the effect of student alienation and poor performance in academic streams:

> A lot of the attendance here is because of the curriculum offered. So a lot do go for the sport. They're there for the sporting side of it. But there's also the other, there's things like retail, they do childcare, all those kind of other things that basically lead into a job. Yeah and a lot of the kids do come for that.
>
> (Julie)

However, as we indicated earlier, differentiated programs and different curriculum pathways can cement inequality (Collins & Yates 2011; Terwel 2005). Through curriculum differentiation and streamed curriculum pathways, schools can create their own structures of inequality by simultaneously creating specific opportunities whilst also closing off others. Moreover, Dalley-Trim et al. (2008) demonstrate that VET subjects are generally perceived by students as 'the poor cousin of real school subjects' within 'the binary logic of knowledge/work, knowing/doing, theoretical/practical and academic/non-academic' (p.67). Of further concern is Klee's suggestion that VET may be perceived 'as a dumping ground for academic failures' (2002, p.53), adding weight to the idea that different curriculum pathways can limit student choices and isolate some students from the full range of school options, as well as abrogate schools' responsibilities to the needs of highly marginalised students.

School based decisions about the curriculum and its capacity to align with a social justice agenda were not confined to the academic and VET pathways alone. The school's leadership team recognised that the associated effects of poverty were much deeper than what could be addressed solely through an approach that simply offered carefully delineated career opportunities. In understanding the many facets of socio-economic disadvantage in the broader community, Crimson High worked with a variety of government and community agencies, investing heavily in its range of support programs, which have now become an integral part of the school curriculum to ensure that all young people were able to attend school and see a place for themselves in the curriculum.

The school employed several ancillary staff–youth workers, health workers, a Student Wellbeing team, and Community Education Counsellors–to give direction to and manage an extensive range of social and emotional wellbeing programs. Some of these programs operated within school class time whilst others were run before or after school and during lunch breaks. As Debra, the youth health nurse, informed us, the school offered these programs as a way to address challenges of early school leavers, child safety and depression. Several programs such as Beyond Blue, Helping Friends, Reach for the Stars, Girls with a Purpose and Power Up provided support for victims of domestic violence, bullying and for young women who were socially disengaged. Some programs, such as their anger management course, became part of the classroom curriculum for all first year students. Other support programs, such as the Young Parents' program and Infant Management program, were organised through a Guidance Officer and Community Health Services to support pregnant and parenting young women and help maintain a link with the school to ensure options for completing their academic studies remained open. Debra also ran health education programs, providing one-on-one consultation and referrals for health intervention. She commented on the success of the program:

> Just having that one session a week with them, [it] has a bit of an impact–not on everyone, but probably around 70 per cent, we do see their engagement at school improve. We do see them settle into school a lot better. . . . We used the statistics of suspensions related to violence, and they had decreased in the two and half years.
>
> (Debra)

Debra's comments highlight the important role that support programs played in the school's efforts to maximise attendance and understand the needs of their students beyond the school environment. Other teachers commented on the need for students to be able to see the connection between school and what motivated them outside of academic study. In this respect, the Sports Excellence programs had a significant pull factor in terms of attracting students who envisaged a sports career for themselves (see Chapter 6). Whilst several people we interviewed talked about the individual successes and the benefits of the school's strong sports program, there was also a concern that students needed to be able to envisage a wide range of options for life beyond school.

The leadership team made it clear that pursuing a social justice agenda also required time to build relationships, not only with the students, their families and community, but also amongst the staff:

> I think that I have more chance of making a difference in education in a place where I've already put in a lot of work, and developed relationships over time. If you really want to change the culture of the place, it's all about developing relationships with people. The leadership team I have has taken me 24 years to develop.
>
> (Geoff)

Building a unified approach and a shared vision amongst the teaching staff is a challenge at a large school such as Crimson High. To this end, the school had an extensive professional development program; it employed two Indigenous liaison workers to support Indigenous students and to train all new teachers in the cultural induction programs they ran. Despite the large number of ancillary staff to enable the range of programs and curriculum pathways, and the mentorship program for all first year teachers, some found their role extremely demanding. Nevertheless, many teachers volunteered to take on some of the support programs that were central to sustaining students' engagement at school. As one teacher told us:

> I'm involved in a program that we have at school, it's called 'Reach for the Stars' and it's a program that we run with girls who are at-risk and are disengaging . . . so I give up one of my spares a week to go and meet with the girls to do that. . . . I think it is [common], especially for teachers who have been here for quite a while and have that passion for kids. For some of the new teachers I think it's very overwhelming. . . .
>
> (Lisa)

The following section considers some of the challenges we have outlined above within the context of developing a differentiated curriculum. We draw on the example of the enacted music curriculum at Crimson High as it highlights the ways in which extracurricular music activities served to engage young people in schooling, while not necessarily the more formal academic curriculum.

Differentiated music curriculum at Crimson High

We became interested in the school's approach to music as a result of the observational work we carried out in lunchtimes at the school. A small room in one of the school buildings had been allocated for our use each time we visited. It could seat approximately 12 people, where we could hold interviews and plan the day's schedule. It was quiet, partly protected from the general noise by a lack of windows, except for the sound of the air conditioning during the hot summer days. We were lucky to have this space, since empty rooms at this large school were scarce. We quickly established a routine, each of us heading out to a classroom to observe lessons, interviewing a teacher or a small group of students each time the bell signalled a change of classes, then returning to our room in the breaks to share our notes. A couple of days had passed before we became aware of the rhythmic drumming occurring in the playground one lunchtime, not far from our room.

A group of approximately a dozen students, mostly boys, were sitting in a circle playing congas and bongos. The rhythmic patterns changed every few minutes, led at first by Ellie, an ancillary staff member, who had initially introduced the drumming circle into the school as a way for struggling students to let off steam, as she later explained. It caught on quickly, and now she was struggling to buy enough drums for the numbers of students wanting to participate. From time to time Ellie would nod to particular drummers in the group to take the lead, then a subtle shift in the pattern would ripple through the group as some of the younger players suddenly realised that the rhythm had changed. Concentration was important, adjusting to the player beside you, listening for emphasis, syncopation, light and shade so that the sound became musical–these were clearly evident for some players and a work in progress for others. Around the drummers stood an even larger group of onlookers. Some of them moved on after a few minutes when it was clear they weren't going to get a turn today, but for the most part they stayed, quite still, absorbed in the moment.

We became interested in the potential of the drumming circle to engage students in the broader curriculum of the school, and in particular with music as a differentiated curriculum area. Through our discussion of the differentiated music curriculum we explored how the school attempted to position itself as a 'school for all'. We have chosen interview extracts to highlight the voices of music students–Jack, Tina and Liam. Their voices suggest that the programs within the music curriculum at Crimson act as a hook to connect with and engage students with the school and to support social learning and a sense of community, as well as academic music skills.

Crimson High offered an extensive music curriculum. The academic stream included classroom music at each Year level, an instrumental program, music extension and enrichment programs, extracurricular music programs, participation in musicals, public community performances, eisteddfods and excursions. There was also a Music Excellence program for students who had reached a relatively high level of competence (instrumental or vocal). In these programs there was an emphasis on developing students' performance skills and ensemble work. The music curriculum also included an informal and extracurricular set of programs in which any student could participate. Some of these were offered through the Pastoral Care program and included extracurricular activities such as musicals and camps. In contrast to the academic stream, these programs primarily focused on the benefits to students' personal growth and development.

Examples of these programs included a recently established boys' choir, talent shows, informal concerts organised by the students themselves or with the help of other teachers, lunchtime guitar classes and the drumming and ukulele groups.

Whilst the informal programs were not, in essence, intended for performance, some of these programs and activities provided opportunities for performances within the school for those wishing to participate. They also provided opportunities for other students to see their peers involved in music-making, promoting confidence and team-building and providing a 'public' performance opportunity in a less-risky context within the school grounds amongst their peers. Our research team happened to be working at the school during a week when one such informal concert evening was scheduled. We took note of the high level of support amongst students and the willingness for students to perform their own compositions or sing a song individually. Taken together all of these opportunities to engage with music-making activities suggested a highly differentiated music curriculum. Within this differentiated music curriculum, students were able to develop their skills and knowledge from their individual point of prior experiences and skill level. In this sense, through their music curriculum, the school appeared responsive to the needs of its students by providing a music curriculum 'for all'.

A differentiated music curriculum as a 'hook': Student perspectives

The music curriculum at Crimson High provided a specific example of how the school attempted to balance the demands of its formal curriculum with its social justice agenda. Here we draw attention to the way the combined formal and informal differentiated music curriculum opened up possibilities for student engagement and for their voices to be heard. We argue that curriculum differentiation can take account of social justice perspectives by asking: 'Whose knowledge and whose voices are privileged?', drawing attention to barriers that may exist for students to both participate and be successful learners in the formal school context.

The music curriculum at Crimson High provided a specific example of how the school attempted to balance the demands of its formal curriculum with its social justice agenda. We outline the ways in which the differentiated set of music programs provided potential for students to engage with the school's academic curriculum, despite their educational disadvantage. We include the voices of music students Jack, Tina and Liam. These students all experienced some difficulties achieving academic success elsewhere in the curriculum, but all shared a love of music. Through their accounts of engagement with music programs at the school, they draw our attention to particular learning experiences which afforded them autonomy and agency. We frame our discussion of these examples within a broader discussion of the roles of the formal and informal curriculum, the 'hooks' that are used to engage students and the pathways that are created, while simultaneously avoiding them becoming corridors to nowhere.

Jack's class timetable included music theory, the newly formed boys' choir and the vocal program which included sight-reading, breathing technique and performance. Jack's commitment to the school musical was extraordinary, and his engagement with many of the school's music programs was a major part of his school life. Jack was struggling with other academic subjects and was receiving extra help to prepare for exams. Balancing the extra hours needed to catch up with his schoolwork with the hours he was working at a local supermarket after school, Jack had limited opportunity to take advantage of all the music programs that were available. However, Jack's participation in the elective and informal music programs demonstrates the powerful hook that extracurricular music programs can be to ensure that young people stay connected to the school community:

> At school, well . . . I've just recently done the musical 'All Shook Up'. . . . Ah, it was great! Well, I didn't go for a lead [role], but just being in the basic stuff was good. . . . So many rehearsals. I think I enjoyed the singing most. . . . It was like every Sunday . . . five hours divided between the singing and dancing. . . . I worked at Woolworths during the time. I had to fit it in. . . . I didn't want to give up the musical. . . . I wanted to learn music, and yeah, like to sing and all that. . . . I used to play–I think my first instrument I played was a little recorder. . . . It was a plastic one. . . . And I think I tried out for euphonium lessons. . . . And I really wanted to join in with the music camps and nights, and learn even more.
>
> (Jack)

Tina also provides an example of the ways in which music had importance in her life. For her, as a student who did not find school easy, the school musical also acted as a means of keeping her engaged with the school. When Tina entered Crimson High, she already had substantial experience with music-making across a range of contexts, and thus the musical was a significant attraction for her:

> At the age of two and a half I was in dancing and from dancing I started singing and from singing I started acting, so it was all linked into one . . . music became my second language. I was able to identify with it. . . . I've got extended, 'adopted' family [and] they hold events like, my neighbours. . . . If they're holding an event, he will be like '[Tina], do you mind doing a gig for me, singing a couple of songs with this background music . . . ?' . . . so I get little gigs just to fill in time. . . . I get paid in free food and drinks. . . . Outside of school, I'm trying to get into musicals the local theatre groups do. I've also done the school musical the last five years.

The school's differentiated music curriculum thus provided Tina a way to transition from home to school and have her skills, experiences and expertise recognised. For both Jack and Tina the social context of learning was very important. Participation in school performances through the choir and musicals provided a space for them to socialise with other students, giving them a sense of belonging in the school. As Jack commented:

> I've got like friends everywhere, but I think most of my friends are in the music department. . . . [Andrew], he's like a conductor now, starting to conduct for co-eds dances. . . . Yeah. My friends, they play instruments, sing–it's awesome, yeah.

Jack's comment about his fellow students reminds us that music-making is essentially a social practice (Bicknell 2009). This social leaning was also identified by other students. For example, Liam commented:

> I think the biggest skill in music is to improvise, and to be able to share with other musicians. Like, be able to not necessarily play on the spot, but be able to sit there with other people, and be able to play together, and feel each other, how they play.

Despite the relatively minor space that improvisation occupies within the formal music curriculum, Liam identified it as relevant to his needs. In order to improvise, Liam had already learnt the requirements of active listening (to other musicians), finding his space within the performance and contributing to the music-making process. His comments reflect Freire's argument that self-reflexive practices are based on the student's own lived experiences that provide both knowledge and the drive for further knowledge (Horton & Freire 1990).

In these extracts we can see how music can help students imagine new possibilities (Young & Muller 2013, p.245). Young's and Muller's discussion of the Arts sits within a debate about access to specialised knowledge as a matter of social justice. They seek, in part, to understand different forms of power within the concept of 'powerful knowledges', rather than analysing the nature of music itself. Where their discussion is useful here is to remind us that powerful knowledges usually reside with the academic, formal curriculum, where there is much at stake in terms of students' future outcomes. However, for these music students their music learning is largely supported by the informal music curriculum at school. Louth (2012) notes the importance of informal learning experiences in shaping personal commitment, arguing that 'the tacit and personal contribution that each person brings to the act of knowing, is an essential element of the overall learning process' (p.18). Further, Griffiths (2012) states that social justice arguments in education are usually framed with reference to future outcomes of disadvantaged students. She suggests instead that a deeper understanding of social justice in education would be gained by understanding the connection between 'joy' and educational experiences, which tend to be investigated more often in relation to the informal curriculum.

The example of the differentiated music curriculum at Crimson High draws attention to the purposes of the curriculum and the hierarchy of knowledges contained within it. Programs such as the drumming circle, as with the school musical, boys' choir and so on, need to be understood within the suite of differentiated programs within the music curriculum at Crimson High. They all work to provide students with knowledge about and skills in music-making. However, they are all differently valued, with the music excellence program carrying the greatest status, and one that typically privileges the already privileged. The primary intent of the non music-excellence programs was not about providing pathways into academic music subjects. As one music teacher explained, students participating in the drumming groups are not the same students who are participating in the music excellence programs. Whilst those students in the latter group are able to join the drumming and ukulele groups, the reverse is not true; that is unless they could pass the audition process, which would usually necessitate extensive instrumental training and family resources. However, for many of the young people we interviewed, such programs do enable them to engage in school and perhaps take up other academic options whilst there. We would thus suggest that the inclusion of a range of informal music programs at this school did provide opportunities, particularly for academically low-achieving students, to re-engage with school and experience deep satisfaction in their learning. Although we are not suggesting that the success of these programs, in terms of student engagement and learning, can be attributed to the music curriculum alone, the school had multiple other programs to keep young people engaged in school. However, by offering a wide range of programs within the music curriculum, both academic and informal, the school provided access to opportunities for music-making for all students, albeit within the limitations of a hierarchy within the music curriculum and the school curriculum more broadly.

As we indicated in Chapter 3, schools, teachers and parents often talk of the high expectations they have for their students. However, in some of the student interviews we conducted with the music students who were struggling in some of their academic curriculum subjects, they were just as articulate about their own expectations in their learning, what they wanted to learn and how they would achieve their goals. During these interviews the music students talked about the connections they made between their home-life and school, finding relevance in what they are learning and also understanding that their learning may offer opportunities to them later in life even if they were not sure what choices they would make. Many of these students also indicated that they had not experienced this type of agency and autonomy at school previously. This may well have been because of the place of music in the curriculum.

The value which music is given in the school curriculum is not easily determined. The formal music curriculum is one that does carry with it high levels of cultural capital, although this is not often read as valuable capital, that is, useful for occupational or university entrance purposes. Thus exploring the differentiated music curriculum at Crimson High does not highlight the same discrepancies of opportunity that might arise from students doing either pre-vocational mathematics or a calculus based mathematics course. However, what it does do is demonstrate that the curriculum is everywhere in a school and that whilst we are concerned that some young people at Crimson High might be missing out on 'powerful knowledges' associated with the academic disciplines, the sense of belonging that arises from such curriculum possibilities engages young marginalised people in schooling, thereby perhaps enabling engagement with more formal and valued aspects of the curriculum.

Conclusion

The lessons from Crimson High demonstrate some of the tensions in trying to address a range of injustices by becoming 'a school for all'. There is no doubt that this inclusive agenda works to ensure that some young people, who would not otherwise be, stay connected to the school. Through a focus on recognitive and representative justice, the school has ensured that differences are taken into account and valued in the differentiated curriculum offerings at Crimson High and by ensuring that diverse voices are heard, including those of students from marginalised backgrounds. However, such efforts, whilst proliferating opportunities for students from marginalised backgrounds, may ignore the hierarchical valuing of knowledge which can exclude some (generally the marginalised students) from access to the powerful knowledges necessary for them to participate in their future social worlds on par with others (Fraser 2009). Such efforts can lead to injustices of maldistribution and a reproducing of the broader inequities of the status quo. This raises key curriculum questions for those who are concerned about social justice and schooling: How do we reconcile such tensions? How do we hook and engage while also broadening and opening up possibilities? How do we value curricular knowledges seen as hooks that engage but go nowhere given that they–as the music curriculum suggests here–support engagement and social learning? How can students' 'funds of knowledge' be employed in ways that value such knowledges whilst also extending the students' worlds?

As we have indicated throughout this book, differentiation is a regular part of school planning and practice. It is often presented as a strategy to address the perceived learning needs of students so that they can achieve success (constructed and enacted in different ways) within the school environment. A differentiated curriculum is no different. The differentiated curriculum at Crimson High worked as a strategy to keep young people engaged with the school. We provided an example of curriculum differentiation, specifically the music curriculum, to interrogate how 'hooks' are used to engage students. However, we have acknowledged that providing a differentiated curriculum is not unproblematic, nor without contradictions. For example, unless those hooks also lead to further opportunities within the formal academic curriculum, pathways can quickly become 'corridors' that lead to nowhere for some.

In the next chapter we focus on the politics of differentiation, culture and Indigeneity at Crimson High. We explore the various approaches of cultural recognition at the school designed to address the high levels of Indigenous disadvantage. We recognise in this chapter the significance of cultural recognition as an important organising principle in struggles for justice but also how it can undermine justice through essentialising cultural difference as other and deficit. In light of this exploration, we argue the importance of educators being critically aware of how they construct race and use it as an organising principle in their work. Through reference to a specific sporting program at the school designed to engage Indigenous boys, we illustrate the imperative of educators understanding culture as an aspect of negotiated social practice rather than a fixed entity.

Notes

1 We have also noted consistent downgrading of the arts in favour of STEM subjects in the UK over the last two years, arguing that they limit students' later employment opportunities; see, for example, statements by UK Secretary for Education in *The Independent* (May 10, 2015) and *The Stage* (November 11, 2014) weekly newspapers.
2 See http://www.australiancurriculum.edu.au/.
3 Summary results of the 2014 *Next Step* survey, a State survey reporting on initial study and work destinations of young people post-school, http://education.qld.gov.au/nextstep/nextstep/2014survey.html.

References

Apple, M 1979, *Ideology and curriculum*. London: Routledge.

Atweh, B & Singh, P 2011, 'The Australian Curriculum: Continuing the national conversation', *Australian Journal of Education* Vol. 55, No. 3, pp. 189–196.

Bicknell, J 2009, *Why music moves us*. Hampshire, UK: Palgrave Macmillan.

Blum, D and Ullman, C 2012, 'The globalization and corporatization of education: the limits and liminality of the market mantra', *International Journal of Qualitative Studies in Education*, Vol. 25. No. 4, pp. 367–373, DOI: 10.1080/09518398.2012.673031.

Brennan, M 2011, National curriculum: A political-educational tangle, *Australian Journal of Education*, Vol. 55, No. 3, Article 7.

Cleaver, D & Riddle, S, 2014, 'Music as engaging, educational matrix: Exploring the case of marginalised students attending an "alternative" music industry school', *Research Studies in Music Education*, Vol. 36, no. 2, pp. 245–256.

Collins, C & Yates, L 2011, 'Confronting equity, retention and student diversity', In L. Yates, C. Collins, and K. O'Connor (Eds.), *Australia's Curriculum Dilemmas: State cultures and the big issues*. Carlton: Melbourne University Press, pp. 107–126.

Dalley-Trim, L, Alloway, N, & Walker, K 2008, 'Secondary School students' perceptions of, and the factors influencing their decision-making in relation to, VET in schools', *The Australian Educational Researcher*, Vol. 35, no. 2, pp. 55–69.

Dunne, M, Humphreys, S, Sebba, J, Dyson, A, Gallannaugh, F and Muijs, D 2007, Effective teaching and learning for pupils in low attaining groups (Nottingham, Research Report DCSF-RR011).

Giroux, H 2010, 'Bare pedagogy and the scourge of neoliberalism: Rethinking higher education as a democratic public sphere', *The Educational Forum*, Vol. 8, no. 6, pp. 715–721.

Gonzalez, L, Moll, N, & Amanti, C (eds) 2005, *Funds of knowledge: Theorizing practices in households, communities, and classrooms*, Lawrence Erlbaum, New Jersey.

Griffiths, M 2012, 'Why joy in education is an issue for socially just policies', *Journal of Education Policy*, Vol. 27 No. 5, pp. 655–670.

Hogan, A, Lingard, B and Sellar, S 2015, 'Edu-businesses and education policy: the case of Pearson'. *Professional Voice*, Vol. 10, No. 2, pp. 24–30.

Horton, M & Freire, P 1990, We make the road by walking: Conversations on education with Myles Horton and Paulo Freire. Philadelphia: Temple University Press.

Hyslop-Margison, EJ, and Sears, AM 2010, 'Enhancing teacher performance: The role of professional autonomy', *Interchange*, Vol. 41, no. 1, pp. 1–15.

Ireson, J, Hallam, S, & Hurley, C 2005, 'What are the effects of ability grouping on GCSE attainment?', *British Educational Research Journal*, Vol. 31, no. 4, pp. 443–458.

Klee, C 2002, 'A practitioner's view of vocational education and training in schools', *Unicorn*, Vol. 28, No. 3.

Louth, P 2012, 'Personhood and Music Learning', In *Personhood and Music Learning: Connecting Perspectives and Narratives*, ed S A O'Neill. Canadian Music Educators' Association.

Luke, A 2010, 'Will the Australian curriculum up the intellectual ante in primary classrooms?', *Curriculum Perspectives*, Vol. 30, no. 3 pp. 59–65.

Lund, D and Carr, P 2008, *Doing democracy: Striving for political literacy and social justice* Peter Lang, New York.

MacAllister, J 2016, What should education institutions be for? *British Journal of Educational Studies*, pp. 1–16. DOI: 10.1080/00071005.2015.1131811.

Macdonald, D, Hay, P and Williams, B 2008, Should you buy? Neo-Liberalism, neo-HPE, and your neo-job. *New Zealand Physical Educator*, Vol. 41, No. 3, pp. 6-14.

McGregor, G & Mills, M 2006, 'RMXing the curriculum: Boys and music education', *Pedagogy, Culture and Society*, Vol. 14, no. 2, pp. 221–233.

The Odyssey of Homer, Available from: https://archive.org/stream. [21 January 2016].

Rata, E 2012, *The politics of knowledge in education*, Routledge Taylor and Francis Group, New York/London.

Sorhagen, NS 2013, 'Early teacher expectations disproportionately affect poor children's high school performance', *Journal of Educational Psychology*, Vol. 105, pp. 465–477.

Terwel, J 2005, 'Curriculum differentiation: Multiple perspectives and developments in education', *Journal of Curriculum Studies'*, Vol. 37, no. 6, pp. 653–670.

Tranter, D 2012, 'Unequal schooling: how the school curriculum keeps students from low socioeconomic backgrounds out of university', *International Journal of Inclusive Education*, Vol. 16, no. 9, pp. 901–916.

Wong, M 2005, 'A cross-cultural comparison of teachers' expressed beliefs about music education and their observed practices in classroom music teaching', *Teachers and Teaching*, Vol. 11, no. 4, pp. 397–418.

Woods, AF, Dooley, KT, Luke, A, & Exley, BE 2014, 'School leadership, literacy and social justice: The place of local school curriculum planning and reform', In *International Handbook of Educational Leadership and Social (In)Justice*, ed I Bogotch & C Shields, Springer, New York, pp. 509–520.

Young, M 2009, 'Education, globalisation and the voice of knowledge', *Journal of Education and Work*, Vol. 22, no. 3, pp. 193–204.

Young, M 2011, 'Curriculum policies for a knowledge society?', In *Curriculum in today's world: Configuring knowledge, identities, work and politics*, ed L Yates & M Grumet, Routledge, London, pp. 125–138.

Young, M 2013, 'Powerful knowledge: An analytically useful concept or just a "sexy sounding term"? A response to John Beck's "Powerful knowledge, esoteric knowledge, curriculum knowledge"', *Cambridge Journal of Education*, Vol. 43, no. 2, pp. 195–198.

Young, M & Muller, J 2010, 'Three educational scenarios for the future: Lessons from the sociology of knowledge', *European Journal of Education*, Vol. 45, no. 1, Part I, pp. 11–27.

Young, M and Muller, J 2013, 'On the powers of powerful knowledge', *Review of Education*, Vol. 1, No. 3, pp. 229–250.

Zipin, L, Sellar, S, & Hattam, R 2012, 'Countering and exceeding "capital": a "funds of knowledge" approach to re-imagining community', *Discourse: Studies in the Cultural Politics of Education*, Vol. 33, no. 2, pp. 179–192.

6 A politics of differentiation and culture

> . . . when is it useful to use the notion of 'Indigenous culture' and 'Aboriginality', and when do these terms cease to become useful and instead work to limit, exclude and contain the possibilities that Indigenous people have for attaining institutional, disciplinary and political capacity?
>
> (McConaghy 2000, p.261)

Working through a politics of differentiation in relation to culture is highly fraught and oftentimes problematic. In our work at both of the research schools we could not help but be impressed by the programs and initiatives that focused on recognising the culture of marginalised groups. Given the high levels of educational disadvantage experienced by the Indigenous students at these schools, many of these programs, as we have already indicated, centred upon the recognition of Indigenous culture, for example, the flagpole initiative at Red Point High and the instating of Acknowledgement of Country practices. Recognising Indigenous culture at Crimson High was a key priority, and there were many and varied programs designed to support this, including extracurricular activities such as the Proud Sisters and football programs, curricular activities such as integrating Indigenous perspectives into various subjects, pedagogical approaches such as storytelling or yarning circles and other programs, for example, mentoring Indigenous students and supporting Indigenous student leadership. These programs were clearly driven by a well-intentioned social justice agenda. In this regard, they were significant in increasing the valuing of Indigeneity through greater cultural recognition and political representation (Fraser 2008). However, our deeper investigation of the politics of differentiation framing this recognition revealed particular complexities and problematics that are captured in the opening quote by McConaghy (2000) in relation to when and how notions of Indigenous culture are useful and when and how they might be limiting. These issues are what we focus on in this chapter.

The significance of culturally responsive schooling in supporting the educational needs of all students, but especially those from marginalised backgrounds, is well recognised across western contexts–including in the United States (Banks 2010; Gay, 2000); Canada (Kanu 2007; Lewthwaite & McMillan 2010); New Zealand (Bishop, 2003; Ritchie 2008), the UK (Ladson-Billings & Gillborn

2004) and Australia (Hayes et al. 2006; Klenowski 2009). Generally, this responsiveness is reflected in teaching and learning that connects with and values the funds of knowledge specific to particular cultural groups. Such teaching and learning are central imperatives of a socially just education–valuing marginalised cultural knowledge can destabilise the hierarchical patterns that create injustices of misrecognition (Fraser 1997). In relation to schooling, it can transform the exclusionary discourses embedded in western (i.e. White, middle class) modes of curriculum, pedagogy and assessment that silence or exclude marginalised learners and compromise their educational outcomes.

There is much evidence to suggest that culturally responsive schooling can improve the participation, motivation and outcomes of marginalised learners (Bishop 2003; Kanu 2007; Klenowski 2009; Sleeter 2005). However, there is also much evidence indicating the tensions and problematics involved in educators' efforts to differentiate on the basis of culture (see Keddie 2012; McConaghy 2000). This chapter explores these possibilities and tensions in relation to one of the case study schools, Crimson High School. We focus on matters of differentiation as they relate to culture and Indigenous disadvantage, as these matters were particularly salient at Crimson High. As we noted in Chapter 1, Crimson High has a relatively high Indigenous population at roughly 25 per cent of all (i.e. 2,300) students and continues to grapple with the racism endemic in the broader community. A key priority at the school is to work against such racism and to ameliorate the educational disadvantage that many Indigenous students at the school experience.

With reference to the school's concerns about Indigenous disadvantage and the various approaches undertaken to address this, we articulate when it may or may not be useful to draw on notions of Indigenous culture as a strategy of recognition. We highlight in this respect how cultural recognition is an important organising principle in struggles for justice (see hooks 1994; Sarra 2003) but also how it can undermine justice through reifying cultural difference as other and deficit (Fraser 2008; Moreton-Robinson 2000). While our focus in this chapter is on Indigeneity, the arguments we offer speak to the complexities of cultural recognition in relation to all marginalised groups. Like the earlier chapters, the politics represented in this chapter bring to light the complexities of differentiation and an absence of consistency in relation to how such differentiation might best be approached. Also consistent with the earlier chapters, our intention here is to highlight possibilities for working in more socially just ways.

We argue in this chapter that such possibilities are enabled by educators being critically aware of how they construct race and use it as an organising principle in their work. This awareness is central to moving beyond the cultural essentialism that tends to predominate within Indigenous education–where cultural reductionism homogenises Indigeneity within and against a dominant White norm. In particular, we argue the imperative of educators understanding culture as an aspect of negotiated social practice rather than a fixed entity. With reference to a specific approach at the school designed predominantly for Indigenous male students–to foster intercultural awareness and respect through sport–we highlight ways in which notions of culturalism and racial incommensurability might be disrupted.

Cultural recognition and Indigenous disadvantage

Creating more equitable societies has been an important mandate of mass education for some time and is reflected in equity policy across the globe. A key concern within western policy discourse relates to raising the schooling participation and achievement of marginalised groups. A familiar theme within such policy is to 'close the gap' in educational outcomes between disadvantaged students and their more advantaged peers. In western contexts such as Australia, Canada and New Zealand, raising the educational performance of Indigenous students has been an important priority–given that Indigeneity is the strongest predictor of educational disadvantage. In these contexts, Indigenous students fall well below their non-Indigenous counterparts on every educational performance measure. Of particular concern in Australia, for example, are Indigenous students' low levels of literacy and numeracy attainment; school attendance and retention rates; and tertiary under-representation (ABS 2006). Such under-performance is associated with the high levels of economic and social disadvantage that continue to plague Indigenous communities. Such under-performance is also associated with the failure of mainstream education to adequately provide for Indigenous students.

Historically, there has been a fundamental disregard for Indigenous traditions, cultures and languages within mainstream (i.e. western) education systems. These systems have been chiefly focused on assimilating Indigenous peoples into non-Indigenous cultures and societies (see Luke 2009; Spring 2003). For many, this lack of regard is exacerbated by the external demands and pressures of the audit culture. While such demands have been positive in highlighting the gravity of Indigenous educational disadvantage and thus the significance of ongoing policy and practice for redressing it, the reductive and data-driven focus of this culture has also been highly negative. Amid its narrow priorities and focus on quantifying and comparing easily measurable testing outcomes, the audit culture has encouraged a static and deficit view of Indigeneity constructed in opposition to (or at odds with) mainstream or conventional education (see Luke 2009; McConaghy 2000; Pearson 2009). As we noted in Chapter 2, these priorities have also led to increasingly narrow and prescriptive teaching and sidelined more qualitatively focused schooling goals–such as moral and social learning.

The Coolangatta Statement on Indigenous Rights in Education (2006) contends that one of the most significant challenges in the ever-changing contemporary world is how best to promote, protect and nurture Indigenous cultures. According to The Statement, this challenge is best addressed through schooling environments that reflect, respect and embrace Indigenous cultural values, philosophies and ideologies (The Coolangatta Statement 1999). This focus is supported in many significant policy initiatives. In Australia, for example, there is strong emphasis on Indigenous cultural awareness in national and state education policy. Cultural inclusion, for example, is prioritised in the National Goals for Schooling Framework. The Framework's particular focus is Indigenous marginality and the role of education in valuing the histories and cultures of this group (MCEETYA 2008). One of the key goals is for schools to support all young Australians to become active and informed citizens who 'understand and acknowledge the value of Indigenous cultures' (p.10). These goals are supported in various curriculum statements nation-wide. Australia's National Curriculum, for example, supports an integration of Aboriginal and Torres Strait Islander histories and perspectives across many of its curriculum areas. The Queensland Education Department's EATSIPS (Embedding Aboriginal and Torres Strait Islander Perspectives in Schools) initiative is another policy that supports schools to embed Indigenous perspectives within the curriculum but also within pedagogy and, more broadly, community engagement and the organisational environment (Queensland Government 2013). Along similar lines to culturally responsive curriculum, 'culturally fair' assessment that is inclusive of Indigenous knowledges is also recognised as important (Klenowski 2009).

Other initiatives have focused on creating more inclusive schooling environments through greater Indigenous staff representation, not always with great success (see Reid & Santoro 2006; Santoro & Reid 2006). In Australia the under-representation of Indigenous teachers (at less than one per cent of all teachers) is seen to be a contributing factor to the poor academic performance of Indigenous students and their low levels of school retention (relative to their non-Indigenous counterparts). There have been initiatives that seek to address this imbalance and increase the number of Indigenous teachers in Australian schools–the aims of this increase are to foster greater cultural awareness and understanding of Indigenous issues and to provide Indigenous students with positive role models within schooling environments that reflect greater autonomy for Indigenous groups (Queensland Department of Education and Training 2011).

While many schools and educators actively endorse these sorts of initiatives and the broader notion of schooling as a vehicle for equity, they tend not to engage in critically examining the assumptions and understandings that shape the way that this notion is played out. Within Indigenous education, as with other minority identity groups, culturalist assumptions have tended to inform equity efforts. McConaghy (2000) defines culturalism as reductionist–where 'culture is seen as a 'knowable, bounded and separate' entity' (2000, p.43, see also Benhabib 2002; Mohanty 2003; Moreton-Robinson 2000). She further explains:

> Culturalism makes appeals to notions of 'tradition' as remote, past and exotic. Cultural identities are stereotypical. Through culturalism, the other becomes naturalised and normalised: we can know they are a real or authentic other, and as a consequence, we can be vigilant to any transgressions of in-authenticity.

According to Benhabib (2002, pp.4–5) this reductionism has 'grave normative political consequences for how we think injustices among groups should be redressed and how we think human diversity and pluralism should be furthered'. Certainly, it denies or erases the complex, dynamic and contingent ways in which cultures are constructed and re-constructed within particular contexts and historical periods. For McConaghy (2000) it is informed by, and re-inscribes, a 'two-race' binary framework (Indigenous/non-Indigenous, traditional/non-traditional, authentic/inauthentic) where 'other' cultures tend to be either inferiorised or unproblematically exalted against a dominant (White/middle class) norm. Within this binary frame, notions of cultural incommensurability have arisen where Indigenous culture is constructed as incompatible or incommensurable with non-Indigenous, or more accurately, 'White' (i.e. Anglo) culture (Donald & Rattansi 1992; McConaghy 2000; Nakata 2007).

In Indigenous education these binaries have tended to manifest in a positioning of cultural relevance (Indigenous knowledges and cultures) in opposition to mainstream schooling (White knowledges and cultures). Even with the more recent, and what some might consider, progressive policy frames promoting intercultural awareness through the integration of culturally inclusive content, there is a sense of cultural reductionism and incommensurability in efforts to distinguish Indigenous culture and knowledge from western culture and knowledge. To be sure, the endlessly ponderable questions raised by McConaghy (2000) in her work–such as: 'What constitutes "western knowledges" and "Indigenous knowledges"?', 'Whose and which knowledges should be privileged?', 'Who can know and speak with respect to these knowledges?' and 'Who can authorise the incorporation of certain knowledge within curricula?' reflect the complexity and perhaps irreconcilability of cultural relevance or inclusion within mainstream education (see also Nakata 2007).

What is clear is that culturally responsive schooling demands that decisions made in relation to these questions are mindful of, and responsive to, the racialised politics specific to school contexts. While policy frames offer schools and educators guidelines for working in culturally inclusive ways, it is evident that there is no one correct way to pursue anti-racist schooling (Dilg 2003; Gillborn 2000; Nieto 1999). As Gillborn (2000, p.476) argues:

> What succeeds at one time, or in one context, may not be appropriate at a later date or in another context. Racism changes: it works differently through different processes, informs and is modified by diverse contemporary modes of representation, and changes with particular institutional contexts. Anti-racism must recognise and adapt to this complexity. In practice this means facing up to the complexities of racism: identifying and combating racism will always be difficult.

With these issues in mind, this chapter highlights the significance of approaches that are mindful of, and responsive to, the racial (in this case Indigenous) politics, relations and experiences within particular schooling contexts. Such approaches must, we argue, reject notions of cultural reductionism and racial incommensurability.

The following presents interview data gathered from administration, teaching and ancillary staff at Crimson High School. We focus on Crimson High here in light of its relatively high Indigenous population and its strong emphasis on addressing Indigenous disadvantage. Through our analysis of the different approaches to cultural recognition at the school, we illustrate the imperative of educators understanding culture as an aspect of negotiated social practice rather than a fixed entity. With reference to a particular approach at the school designed predominantly for the Indigenous male students, we draw attention to the ways in which notions of culturalism and racial incommensurability might be disrupted. This is the key emphasis within critical anti-racism education, where working with 'difference' means working with complex, non-stereotypical and dynamic identity constructions 'and 'talking to' the actual ways in which people experience their lives, worlds, and identities' (Carrim & Soudien 1999, p.154). Our contention in this chapter is that such ways of working are crucial in moving beyond simplistic versions of culturally responsive teaching (i.e. that connect superficially with the funds of knowledge and experience that might resonate with a particular cultural group). As much research in this area argues (see Banks 2010; Bishop 2003; Gay 2000; Hingangoroa Smith 2003; Lewthwaite & McMillan 2010), this version of 'responsiveness', consistent with McConaghy's notion of culturalism, can be highly problematic–with presumptions of cultural homogeneity likely to lead to the further 'othering' of non-dominant cultures. Consistent with this research, we advocate a more critical approach that does not deploy fixed notions of culture but engages contextually with marginalised knowledges and experiences towards creating more meaningful and relevant learning encounters for marginalised students.

Supporting Indigeneity at Crimson High

Crimson High is well recognised within its local and broader community as providing strong educational and social support for Indigenous students. Key to this support is an explicit valuing of Indigenous cultures. The school's approach to cultural recognition is explored here through the voices of nine members of the Crimson High staff: the non-Indigenous principal, 'Geoff', the non-Indigenous deputy principal, 'Wendy', Indigenous community liaison workers, 'Rhonda', 'Jane' and 'Cynthia', and non-Indigenous teachers, 'Sandy', 'Adam', 'Katrina' and 'Alison'. Like most schools in Australia, as we noted in Chapter 1, Crimson High's staff demographic was overwhelmingly female, White and middle class. While there were Indigenous staff at the school, they were few and limited to the ancillary staff. The following sections are organised around the issues detailed earlier and reflect the ways in which the data were analysed. The first sections foreground the educators' concerns about the key factors constraining the schooling outcomes of Indigenous students, namely poor attendance and achievement, and the strategies at the school designed to address these concerns (e.g. based on cultural inclusion or recognition and Indigenous representation). The subsequent section examines some of the tensions associated with the constructions of race/Indigeneity framing these concerns, namely relating to culturalism and racial incommensurability. The final section refers to a specific approach at the school that reflects potential in terms of disrupting notions of culturalism and racial incommensurability.

In this chapter we represent the voices of both Indigenous and non-Indigenous educators. As race and class-privileged researchers investigating the racialised politics within a White (i.e. Anglo-Australian) governed institution, we are mindful of the problematics involved in representing Indigenous voices. Certainly, such representation is vulnerable to reflecting the imperialism and paternalism that many Indigenous groups remain highly critical of in their view of texts written about them rather than by them or with them (see Moreton-Robinson 1998; 2000). Notwithstanding the importance of this criticism, we are more concerned in this chapter with the problematics that can arise from bio-deterministic assumptions about voice and representation–where an individual's membership to a certain identity group is seen as a literal determinant of their knowledge and actions in relation to the group (see Spivak 1990) and where it is assumed that an individual needs to be a member of a particular group to authentically represent the interests of the group (Keddie 2012; McConaghy 2000).

We position these assumptions as problematic in linking voice or representation to identity in reductionist ways. Such representation, whatever identity relation it might refer to (whether regarding inequities associated with race, ethnicity, gender, sexuality or religion for example) drastically simplifies group identity. It restricts who can know and speak about issues of marginality and ignores the productive and important role that members of privileged groups must play to support marginalised groups. It also places undue expectation and responsibility on members of marginalised groups to authentically represent, and act on behalf of, the interests of their group while also delimiting their opportunities to know and speak about things other than matters associated with their marginality (see Moreton-Robinson 2000). We agree with McConaghy (2000, p.2) here when she contends that:

> . . . we should resist the fashion to prescribe that only Indigenous people can know and speak about Indigenous issues. The links between racialised identity, knowledge and legitimacy can no longer be sustained within either imperialist or anti-imperialist projects.

We thus take the view that marginalised voices are complex and multifaceted and, while they might represent the interests of a particular group, they will not necessarily engage in anti-racist politics of the kind advocated in this chapter–they will, for example, sometimes engage in the culturalism and racial incommensurability that are presented here as reproducing racialised inequities/binaries. In no way, however, is our critique intended to undermine the significance of Indigenous representation in schools–we strongly advocate such representation. Our view, as we illustrate in the following sections, is that such representation, while warranted, is not unproblematic and must be subject to critical scrutiny (as indeed should all forms of identity-related group representation). Such scrutiny, we contend, is all the more important given the renewed emphasis in Australia and other western nations on increasing Indigenous staff representation in schools and the danger in such emphasis of homogenising, or making reductionist assumptions about, Indigenous voices.

Issues of concern

Consistent with the statistics delineating the key aspects of Indigenous educational disadvantage, poor school attendance and its association with academic under-achievement were the major concerns staff articulated in relation to the school's Indigenous students. Geoff's comments were illustrative:

> Indigenous kids don't perform as well academically, and they don't attend as much. Our Indigenous attendance data, there's a big gap. So there's a huge job to be done . . . it doesn't matter what program you use–if they don't come to school, nothing's going to work. So that's got to be the first priority, to get everyone to school.

Following these concerns, a central priority at Crimson High is to raise Indigenous students' attendance but also, as Geoff further remarked, to engage and motivate these students–as he stressed: 'of course you've got to get them to want to come to school . . . there's got to be something here for them'. There was strong agreement amongst staff that education is the key to ameliorating the circumstances of disadvantage that many Indigenous students are born into. For Wendy, education was a way to 'help Indigenous students to see that their life [and their community] can be different' and 'ultimately more positive'. On this issue, one of the Indigenous workers in the school, Rhonda, reflected on her father's instilling of the value of education as a way out of the generational poverty and hardship that had faced their family:

> . . . [my dad], he's 82 now. He had to go to work at 14 . . . to feed his family and keep his mum alive. . . . He always instilled in the kids you have to have a good education, you don't want a shit job. You get in, put your head down, bum up and do education and everything. It's what you put in is what you're going to get out.

Consistent with the view of education within these remarks and the policy initiatives outlined earlier, there were many programs and practices at Crimson High that sought to address the disadvantages confronting the Indigenous students. These programs/practices, importantly, reflected a multidimensional approach to equity–especially in attempting to remove some of the cultural and political barriers impeding these students' educational success (Fraser 1997; 2009). There was a strong emphasis, for example, on cultural awareness in the form of recognising significant Indigenous days and ceremonies, as Rhonda explained:

> . . . there is a lot of support in the school . . . we're big on having traditional dancing at the school and NAIDOC [National Aboriginal and Islander Day

> of Observance Committee] week . . . we're quite lucky here 'cause the executive up top there, they're very, very for acknowledging the traditional owners and 'Welcome to Country' and that, so we're very fortunate here.

As well as generating awareness, appreciation and respect for Indigenous culture in the general student body, such recognition was seen to be particularly positive in supporting the Indigenous students to feel a sense of pride in their cultural heritage and a positive connection to other Indigenous students. Geoff commented, for example, on a dance performance as part of the school's observance of NAIDOC where an older Indigenous boy mentored a younger Indigenous boy:

> That was the best performance we saw yesterday because the guy who was leading them, they had practice sessions, I was there a couple of times, he got up and said things like 'This is about our culture, and don't muck it up'. Some of the kids would stop. And the little boy, who is in Grade 8, he's been in some significant trouble recently, the fact that he [was doing this] did his self-esteem a lot of good, and the fact is that he takes direction from . . . the older boy.

In relation to cultural awareness, there was also strong emphasis on integrating Indigenous perspectives and knowledges within the formal curriculum. This integration tended to be referred to within the context of broader policy mandates such as those identified earlier. In addition to the Indigenous Studies classes at the school within the SOSE [Studies of Society and Environment] curriculum where, for example, the junior students created an Indigenous bush garden, there were explicit attempts to integrate Indigenous perspectives and knowledges across all learning areas. For instance, in 'Marine Aquatic Practices' Sandy supported students to 'look at traditional Indigenous techniques and the sea-food industry', and in mathematics Adam challenged the notion that 'Indigenous people don't have a maths system' with his introduction of the Indigenous base 5 system of numeracy notation to juxtapose against other systems such as the Babylonian base 60 and the European base 10.

These endeavors are highly generative examples of culturally inclusive and relevant teaching practice–connecting with the histories, cultures, contributions and perspectives specific to marginalised groups in such a manner can support greater participation, motivation and achievement for students from these groups (see, for example, Banks 2010; Bishop 2003; Gay 2000; Sleeter 2005). Such connectedness is important in disrupting the cultural exclusivity within western teaching that privileges White and middle class ways of knowing and being and marginalises 'other' ways of knowing and being. It is central to opening a space for more equitable patterns of cultural recognition to be generated that reflect greater respect and esteem for marginalised groups (Fraser 1997).

There was also a strong focus at Crimson High on Indigenous representation. With the aim of enhancing the school's connection to its Indigenous community towards greater student attendance and engagement, the school employed a number of Indigenous ancillary staff, including three community liaison workers

(Cynthia, Jane and Rhonda). Alongside their important liaison role between Indigenous students' home and school environments, these workers also supported staff cultural awareness with their involvement in various professional development and induction programs and their support on integrating and respecting Indigenous perspectives and knowledges within curricula and extracurricular activities. Katrina expressed her view about the value these workers represented in relation to their knowledge about some of the Indigenous students:

> . . . particularly with last year I had a [class with a] high Indigenous student body . . . [Cynthia] helped me, working with her actually helped me a lot to get to know some things that you would not necessarily . . . [Cynthia] would tell me things and she got to know the kids a lot better too, because I guess she was more approachable to the kids than what I was as the teacher. So, I think that helped. Working with [Cynthia and Jane] . . . like, if you have any issues, just say 'hey I've got a problem' or 'can you help chase this up?' because they do home visits and things like that as well. So they have a better understanding of the kids than sometimes we do and we can access that, so that helps.

The Community Liaison Workers also adopted an advocacy role for students in relation to behavioural/discipline issues. Indigenous representation was further supported through the school's Indigenous leadership program and the election of Indigenous school captains. While wary of charges of tokenism, Geoff described this as an important statement of respect to 'show leadership amongst the Indigenous students'. He was particularly thrilled that the elected male school captain, open to all senior boys, was also Indigenous (as with Red Point High). For Rhonda the captaincy was something for the 'kids to strive towards'. There were other initiatives at Crimson High designed to represent Indigenous voices, for example, an Indigenous parents' group involving the three liaison workers where, according to Wendy, parents can 'come along' and discuss any 'issues or things that they want us to develop'.

These sorts of practices and programs are highly generative in beginning to address some of the circumstances of disadvantage confronting Indigenous students. They are productive responses to the broader policy mandates referred to earlier. However, working to support Indigenous equity is a highly complex process that is informed by particular ways of thinking about race and culture that are often taken-for-granted and unconsciously mobilised. It is crucial then to examine the politics within which such inclusive and anti-racist schooling practices are situated (Gillborn 2000). The following illuminates some of these complexities and, in particular, the sense of culturalism and racial incommensurability that framed some of the thinking about Indigeneity at Crimson High.

Culturalism and racial incommensurability

As suggested earlier, education at Crimson High is seen to be the key to supporting Indigenous students to take up more positive futures. This was a view that was strongly expressed by Jane, Rhonda and Cynthia towards students' overcoming the generational poverty and disadvantage many were born into. However, doing well at school seemed to be constructed as counter to Indigenous culture. The following comments from Jane illuminate this. In the two data snippets below, she refers to the school's cohort of 'Island People' (people not from the Torres Strait but from a nearby Island)–whose children often relocated to the mainland to attend Crimson High. This Island originally served as a reserve created by the Queensland State government (from the 1920s) to isolate those Indigenous people who were deemed 'disruptive' or unlawful. It is now an independent Aboriginal shire (since the mid-1980s), but remains troubled with very high levels of welfare dependency and disenfranchisement. She stated:

> A lot of the Island People, they want them to do well but they also don't want them to lose their culture so they do keep that fairly strong. One of [our students] . . . he came from the Island when he was 1. He got to 15 and said, 'I want to go back to find out where I'm from' . . . and I said, 'Absolutely if you want to go back there later that's fine, but do not go back there and be a bum'. I said, 'You need to take something back to your community. Go back as an electrician or a plumber, builder or something, you know? . . . something that you can take back to the community and add to it' . . . and I say, 'You can't go and be a burden on a community because then you've wasted all the opportunities in education that you had here'.
>
> With loving your family you've got to say 'but I don't like this way of living. What can I do to improve myself?' But it's a hard rut to get out of. They're grabbing you by the legs to pull you back and saying you know, 'this is your culture and stay longer and learn your dances and your cultural things'. But you need someone there pushing them up and saying, 'get out there and get an education'.
>
> (Jane)

In these remarks there is a sense of culturalism and racial incommensurability where Indigeneity is constructed and understood within a two-race binary framework (McConaghy 2000). Jane's reference to the 'Island People' suggests that there is an authentic and knowable Island culture that in their eyes is threatened with their children's exposure to mainland/mainstream (i.e. White) schooling culture. For the Islanders (at least from Jane's perspective), this culture must be recognised and preserved through, for example, the new generations learning their dances and 'cultural things' for fear of 'los[ing] their culture'. It is clear that: 1) recognising and, indeed, preserving such cultural knowledges are significant in supporting equity for the Indigenous (Islander) students at Crimson High (akin to the cultural awareness strategies noted earlier that recognise group identity as an important organising principle in struggles for justice, see hooks 1994; Sarra 2003) and 2), as noted in Chapter 1, that schools have not done this well–thereby verifying the 'fears' the Islanders express about losing their culture within White-governed institutions that have paid little respect to it. It is also clear, however, that such constructions of culture *can* be problematic. For instance, they can work to simplify and deny the rich complexities, multiplicities and contradictions of Indigenous identities (Fraser 2009; Moreton-Robinson 2000) and especially the new cultural expressions that young Indigenous people might embrace. Such constructions of minority culture (as authentic, unique and natural), moreover, position social change as a betrayal to minority group culture and tradition. These constructions have been strongly challenged in their assumption that, while majority culture can change, innovate and endure the tensions created by modernity, minority culture lacks the capacity to endure these tensions and must adhere to 'known cultural patterns' (Tamir 1999, p.51, see also, Anthias 2002; McConaghy 2000).

In these comments, furthermore, this idea of culture is positioned in binary opposition to, and incommensurable with, mainstream education, as Jane states: 'they [the Island people] want them to do well but they also don't want them to lose their culture'. Islander culture is homogenised and inferiorised at least by inference with Jane's remarks: 'don't go back there and be a bum' or a 'burden' and 'they need someone pushing them up'. These comments are produced within a frame that privileges the resources gained from mainstream education–e.g. being a plumber or builder. Here 'giving back' and 'adding' to the community are constructed as enabled through the taking up of non-Indigenous, rather than Indigenous, ways of knowing and being. It is important to acknowledge that there are opportunities and resources that Indigenous students can and should gain through their involvement in mainstream education. It is also important to locate these remarks within the context of the Island's troubled colonial/penal history–where different Indigenous groups were forced together and detached from their varying communities and places of origin–creating ongoing tensions and conflicts between families and groups. The situation and prospects on the Island for the students are, in many ways, bleak given this history of oppressive colonialism. The comments about students 'taking something back' to their community, not being a 'bum' or 'burden' must be read within this context–especially given the Island's current status as an Aboriginal shire and the responsibility this independence would represent for new Islander generations to 'give back' and 'add' to their community.

Nonetheless, it is also important to recognise the problematics of the culturalism informing these remarks. The binaries of Indigenous/non-Indigenous tend to essentialise and normalise the otherness and marginality of Indigeneity and the centrality and privilege of non-Indigeneity or Whiteness, fortifying a sense of cultural incompatibility that in many ways reproduces, rather than disrupts, racial inequities and binaries (see McConaghy 2000; Moreton-Robinson 2000).

Another issue at Crimson High that reflected a sense of culturalism within a two-race binary frame was the charges of racism deployed by some Indigenous students towards some staff members. Many of the staff expressed concern about this issue, as the following comments from Sandy, Adam and Alison illustrate:

> A lot of kids push your buttons at this school, and if you tell them to do something, they'll turn around and say, 'Oh, is it because I'm Black?'
>
> (Sandy)

> The Indigenous kids are quick to cry racist. 'You don't like me because I'm Black'. It's like, well that's got nothing to do with it. Three of my kids are Black. You know, like, I don't like your behaviour . . . some of the kids I've encountered have been quick to cry racist when . . . and it's not just between student and teacher, it's between student and student as well. You know, 'you don't like me because . . .' or 'you won't sit next to me because . . .'
>
> (Adam)

> We had a few clashes over a few things, like sometimes, with Indigenous students, if they feel that you're . . . picking on them, and then they make the comment that it's because you might be racist. There was that type of thing . . . I find it very upsetting because I'm not racist. It's not fair. I'm just expecting you to do it because that's the rule!
>
> (Alison)

In these comments, as with Jane's earlier remarks, there is a racialised pitting of 'Blackness' against 'Whiteness' in her account of the students' 'cries' of racism. Such accounts essentialise race difference and produce relations of Indigenous and non-Indigenous incommensurability. While it is, of course, imperative to identify and address all instances of racism, these comments suggest that some Indigenous students at Crimson High may be reducing problems not necessarily solely attributable to matters of race or culture to these matters (see Keddie & Niesche 2012). Given the importance placed on Indigenous equity at Crimson High and the severity associated with addressing/sanctioning racism, it seems, indeed, that students' can 'push buttons' through accusing staff of racism. Such accusations–and the cultural reductionism/incommensurability undergirding them–might be seen then as a useful strategy of power in students' relationships with teachers to avoid particular directives or sanctions.

Disrupting notions of culturalism and racial incommensurability

Importantly, the educators at Crimson High expressed sensitivity to the Indigenous politics within the school and the broader community that generate such issues and relations of culturalism. In particular, their reflection on expressions of Indigeneity acknowledged their construction in resistance to White domination (see Moreton-Robinson 2000). Many of the staff, for example, noted the long and troubled history of Indigenous/White relations within the community and spoke against the regular instances of 'racism and resentment' arising from these tensions. Rhonda noted, for example, that 'people's lack of understanding' meant that many in the community unfairly and inaccurately equated Indigenous kids with gang culture and crime. Akin to Phil's account of the racism surrounding Red Point High becoming a 'Black School' (see Chapter 3), Geoff spoke further of the ways in which racism and resentment towards Indigenous people in the community impacted on the school:

> There's been a community reaction to the growth of the Indigenous population in our school. We used to have about 60 to 80 kids for many many years. Our Indigenous population has grown only in the last six or eight years, to the extent it has. We had 450 last year. It's about 20 per cent or 22 per cent of our total population. So it's very significant. And I know when that was happening, there were teachers who said 'there are too many Black kids', and there were people in the community–if they saw 3 or 4 Indigenous kids walking home together–they would think there was a Black riot on . . . we did start to get a name as a big Black school. That has destroyed a number of schools in this town [with] big Indigenous populations, they got known as the 'Blackfella Schools', and no-one would go to them . . . there are principals around who see their major educational job as keeping the 'rubbish' out.

Geoff's view was that the school had 'overcome' the negative connotations associated with 'Blackfella Schools' through its many programs and initiatives designed to recognise and value Indigenous perspectives and cultures. Thus, the school's explicit focus on developing pride in Indigeneity responded to, and against, the racism within the broader community. Such ways of thinking, importantly, appreciate the significance of recognising and preserving specific Indigenous cultural traditions–so important to the Islander people (as articulated in Jane's earlier comments).

It is also important, however (as this chapter has argued), to guard against the homogenising of culture that can arise from this focus on cultural recognition or valuing. Importantly, Geoff's location of Indigeneity within broader racialised politics enables culture to be understood as an aspect of negotiated practice rather than an 'already-read' and fixed entity (McConaghy 2000). For Moreton-Robinson (2000, p.14) it is this thinking that opens spaces for understanding the cultural specificities of Indigenous people's lives as 'enmeshed in historically constructed relations with White people that continue to inform processes of inter-subjectivity in Indigenous and White cultural domains'. It enables 'cries' of racism, for example, to be understood within the town's colonial history where wariness towards White institutions (such as Crimson High) is to be expected. Such cries within this context can thus be seen as an aspect of social practice enmeshed in historically constructed relations with White people.

These situated understandings of Indigeneity are central to disrupting the negative impacts of culturalism and racial incommensurability. At Crimson High such understandings were evident in some of the descriptions educators offered about particular strategies they found useful for fostering students' intercultural awareness and respect for each other. One that seemed highly generative related to how the school addressed the hostilities between the Indigenous and Maori male students. Crimson High attracted many Indigenous students to its sporting programs and, in particular, its football program, which involved many of the school's Indigenous boys. According to many staff, this program was instrumental in raising these boys' engagement with school and their sense of self-esteem. Indeed, sporting programs more broadly have been important mechanisms in

Australia for Indigenous males in this respect for some time (see Hallinan & Judd 2012).

Hostilities between the school's Indigenous boys and some Maori boys arose at Crimson High when this Indigenous space was threatened by the inclusion of Maori boys; as Wendy explained, 'the Indigenous kids felt that these boys were taking their place and there was resentment in the school and the community'. While not deploying a two-race binary frame where Blackness is pitted against Whiteness (as presented earlier), this conflict seemed to homogenise and pit 'Black against Black', to use Jane's terminology, because it occurred between Indigenous and Maori students:

> [a lot of conflict] has been Black on Black for want of a better way to put it. When I started here . . . we had a big problem with the Maoris vs. the Murris [Queensland Aboriginal people] of the Black kids. . . .
>
> (Jane)

According to Wendy, the school had to 'work hard' to foster a sense of reconciliation of this conflict, especially (presumably) given the significant tensions between these two communities within the broader township–and indeed, reflected in many communities across Australia. Geoff referred to sport 'if done properly' as an important 'educator' to foster reconciliation, and this was the vehicle at Crimson High that was drawn on to address the conflict between these groups in ways that fostered intercultural awareness and respectful relations. The sports program worked in conjunction with other programs, such as the Indigenous leadership scheme (where older boys mentored younger boys) and mediation sessions with the Indigenous Community Workers (that, according to Jane, challenged ignorance and prejudice through a focus on the commonalities between the students' different cultural backgrounds). This conjunction was focused on identifying and addressing issues of concern (such as the hostilities between Indigenous and Maori students) in multifaceted and collaborative ways.

In terms of being 'done properly', Geoff explained that sport in the curriculum was more than 'playing games'; it taught the boys to 'be in a team', to have 'self-respect' and to 'look after your mates'. He further elaborated on this point with reference to a particular incident during a football trip with the boys:

> . . . we worked hard. I think sport is a great equaliser . . . I'm very involved in the leadership camp, and the rugby league program. We went away with a group of [25] boys . . . so we had a night to spare, so we all sat down in the hotel room, and I said 'Let's talk about where we all come from'. It was quite incredible. Everyone spoke openly about their background. We had Aboriginals [sic], we had Islanders, we had Papua New Guineans, we had people from the South Sea Islands, we had Maoris; we had all sorts of people. There was one boy, for example, who said he had never ever known his Mum and Dad, because it was in their culture, they were given away. Everyone was just [silent] and people treated him differently the next day because they knew him differently. Amongst those boys, there was a tremendous bond

> and they cared for one another and I see that in the football team . . . [for example] one thing they would never have done, they sleep together [on camp] . . . the Black kids and the White kids do. . . . It's an example of the sort of bond that those fellas had. I think sport, if it's done properly is . . . we don't just have sport in terms of playing games. We try to use sport as an educator, because the people in this community love sport. If you want to know about our community, they're nuts about sport–and rugby league, in particular.

Just as with the programs and initiatives articulated earlier organised specifically around Indigenous identity (e.g. the celebration of Indigenous days), this approach to sport at the school aligns with a multidimensional equity focus, especially in its capacity to support cultural and political justice–that is, it positively values the culture of these Indigenous boys and it provides a context where they can enjoy a sense of autonomy. Importantly, and also consistent with the earlier examples, this approach reflects a pedagogy of 'caring'–which is a culturally responsive pedagogy that combines social support with high expectations and is, according to Gay (2000), requisite to enhancing the educational experiences and outcomes of culturally marginalised students. Certainly, such a pedagogy seems to resonate with the school's general approach to Indigenous issues and engagement and is clearly instrumental in its success at engaging Indigenous students.

While, to these ends, all of the strategies at Crimson High designed to support Indigenous students are likely to be (variously) productive, the approach to sport at the school is less vulnerable to the negative impacts of culturalism and racial incommensurability that can arise from programs and initiatives that focus on articulating or preserving a distinctly Indigenous culture or identity–that can be pitted against White or other identities. The sports program focuses, rather, on connecting with cultural expressions of Indigenous male identity (i.e. sporting prowess) that are currently important to many of the Indigenous boys at Crimson High (as well as representing high status in the community) to foster greater intercultural awareness and respectful relations amongst many different cultural groups.

Rather than recognising Indigenous or non-Indigenous identity simply on the basis of privilege/opportunity or marginality/lack of opportunity (McConaghy 2000), this approach mobilises a group identity around cultural expressions that are not delineable to a particular racial/ethnic group. In this context, sport as an 'educator' reflects potential to create a safe and respectful context that recognises the boys' complex and multifaceted cultural backgrounds and identities towards 'knowing' and 'treating' each other 'differently'. It is important to acknowledge here that there are many aspects of football culture that are highly problematic in re-inscribing harmful versions of masculinity–as is well recognised in the literature on sport, masculinity and violence (see Messner 1992; Hickey 2008). Hickey's work (2008) captures well this problematic when he argues that football culture in its valuing of hardness, solidarity and stoicism, can lead to hyper-masculine cultures of entitlement, abuse and exclusion. Other work in this area of masculinity and sport, while highlighting the complexity of the intersections between gender, race, ethnicity and football (Kearney 2012), has tended to associate marginality in terms of race with fueling hyper-masculine cultures (see Messner 1992; Mills 2001). For marginalised boys and men, as Mills argues (2001), football can provide an arena for accruing societal respect that would otherwise not be forthcoming. In relation to Maori cultures, Horton (2014) has argued that the power, aggression and combat of rugby have become important rites of passage to manhood and even a substitute for the traditional warrior initiation in both Australian and Pasifika contexts. And in relation to Indigenous Australian males, football can, in Kearney's view (2012, p.946), provide a 'ticket for entry into a category of masculinity that remains dominated by White heterosexual males, the perceived and very real locus of power in Australia'.

Notwithstanding these problematics, the account of football at Crimson High that Geoff provides reflects the *potential* of this space to support alternative constructions of masculinity and race/ethnicity towards fostering, in his words, 'tremendous bonds' based on 'care' and intercultural respect. Importantly, using sport as an educative space along these lines, it is possible to avoid the culturalism and racial incommensurability that continue to undermine culturally responsive schooling initiatives/programs. This space reflects an understanding of culture as an aspect of negotiated social practice–absent here are assumptions that there is an authentic or knowable Indigenous identity. Instead there is a recognition of the cultural expressions important, but not solely attributable to, particular Indigenous students. Also absent is an isolation or binary pitting of one culture or race against another culture or race.

Conclusion

Commitment to improving the educational outcomes of Indigenous students is a key policy imperative in western contexts such as Australia. While most educators in these contexts embrace such commitment, they tend not to engage in critically examining the assumptions and understandings that shape how this notion is played out. Consistent with important anti-racist work (see Gillborn 2000), this chapter has highlighted the significance of educators' critical awareness of how they construct race and use it as an organising principle in their work. This awareness, we contend, is requisite in moving beyond the notions of culturalism and racial incommensurability that homogenise Indigeneity within and against dominant White norms. Such awareness, when drawing on an understanding of culture as an aspect of negotiated social practice rather than a fixed entity, opens spaces for a critical anti-racism that works with complex, non-stereotypical and dynamic constructions of identity and 'difference' and responds to the actual ways in which people experience their lives, worlds and identities (Carrim & Soudien 1999).

At Crimson High, such awareness was reflected in educators' sensitivity to the racialised politics impacting on the school that worked to undermine the educational performance of Indigenous students, for example, resistance from teachers and the community associated with Crimson High, and other schools in the area, being seen as 'Blackfella' schools and the regular instances of 'racism and resentment' within the community towards Indigenous people. The school's response to overcoming such racism was the implementing of programs and initiatives based on recognising and valuing Indigenous cultures and perspectives. Programs and initiatives fostering cultural recognition (in the form of recognising significant Indigenous days and ceremonies) and political representation (through ensuring Indigenous staff were consulted in matters concerning Indigenous students) to these ends were extremely significant. However, as this chapter argued, such recognition and representation does not necessarily promote an anti-racist politics that rejects notions of culturalism and racial incommensurability.

Mindful of, and responsive to, the racial politics within the school and broader community, we foregrounded the potential of the sports program at Crimson High to reflect such a politics. Designed to address the hostilities between the Indigenous and Maori male students, sport played an educative role at the school–it was about teaching the boys teamwork, self-respect and looking after each other towards greater intercultural awareness and respectful relations. Geoff's account of the football trip illuminated the potential of this space to support cultural recognition and political representation–it reflected a valuing of the expressions of culture important to (many of) the Indigenous boys at Crimson High as well as providing a context where these boys enjoyed a sense of autonomy. We drew attention to the potential of this program to destabilise the notions of culturalism and racial incommensurability that tend to predominate within culturally responsive schooling. This context offered scope to explore some of the rich complexities, multiplicities and contradictions of Indigenous (and other marginalised) identities. While, indeed, culturally responsive, this program does not presume a static or authentic Indigenous culture that is knowable and delineable to this group. Rather it focuses on connecting with particular expressions of Indigeneity that are significant to many of the Indigenous boys at Crimson High, thus recognising the new cultural expressions that these boys are embracing as part of their Indigeneity.

We are not suggesting in this chapter that sports programs like the one at Crimson High can be a substitute for initiatives in schools that draw on, and positively recognise, Indigeneity as an identity marker. This identity marker remains an important organising principle in struggles for justice and is imperative in pursuing cultural recognition and political representation for Indigenous people. We are arguing that working to support Indigenous equity is a highly complex process and that strategies in this endeavor (especially those mobilised around a group identity politics) can undermine anti-racism through ascribing to notions of culturalism and racial incommensurability. Given this, our contention is that all strategies purporting to be inclusive or anti-racist must critically engage with the politics within which they are situated towards challenging and transforming these notions whether, as at Crimson High, they be endemic in the community, unconsciously mobilised through staff members' assumptions about Indigenous and non-Indigenous culture and identity or deployed by Indigenous students as a strategy of power in their relationships with White teachers.

There is no one correct way to pursue anti-racist or culturally responsive schooling. There are times, as McConaghy (2000) argues, when it is entirely appropriate to draw on notions of 'Indigenous culture' to enable possibilities for Indigenous people just as there are times when such notions work to limit and exclude these possibilities. What is clear is that rejecting notions of culturalism and racial incommensurability must be a central part of this endeavor.

In the next chapter we draw together the key findings of the book. We focus on the significance that particular contextual factors at Red Point High and Crimson High played in relation to each school's engagement with a politics of differentiation for social justice. The chapter culminates in a set of provocations that are based on the book's primary insights. These provocations seek to proliferate new lines of thought and enquiry about how differentiation might be framed within schools to better align with social justice goals.

References

Anthias, F 2002, 'Where do I belong?': Narrating collective identity and translocational positionality', *Ethnicities*, Vol. 2, no. 4, pp. 491–514.

Australian Bureau of Statistics (ABS) 2006, 'Indigenous statistics for schools', In *The Coolangatta Statement on Indigenous People's Australian Bureau of Statistics*, The Government of Australia. Available from: http://www.abs.gov.au. [22 July 2009].Banks, J 2010, 'Multicultural education: Characteristics and goals', In *Multicultural education: Issues and perspectives*, ed J Banks & C Banks, John Wiley and Sons, New Jersey, pp. 3–30.

Benhabib, S 2002, *The claims of culture: Equality and diversity in the global era*, Princeton University Press, Princeton, NJ.

Bishop, R 2003, 'Changing power relations in education: Kaupapa Māori messages for "mainstream" education in Aotearoa/New Zealand', *Comparative Education*, Vol. 39, no. 2, pp. 221–238.

Carrim, N & Soudien, C 1999, Critical antiracism in South Africa'. In *Critical multiculturalism: Rethinking multicultural and antiracist education*, ed S May, Falmer Press, London, pp. 153–171.

Department of Education and Training 2011, *Embedding aboriginal and Torres Strait Islander Perspectives in schools*, State of Queensland. Available from: www.deta.qld.gov.au. [1 July 2012].

Dilg, M (ed) 2003, *Thriving in the multicultural classroom: Principles and practices for effective teaching*, Teachers' College Press, New York.

Donald, J & Rattansi, A 1992, 'Introduction', In *'Race', Culture and Difference*, ed J Donald & A Rattansi, Sage Publications, London, pp. 1–10.

Fraser, N 1997, *Justice interruptus: Critical reflections on the 'postsocialist' condition*, Routledge, New York.

Fraser, N 2008, 'Rethinking recognition: overcoming displacement and reification in cultural politics', In *Adding insult to injury: Nancy Fraser debates her critics* ed K Olson, Verso, London, pp. 129–14.

Fraser, N 2009, *Scales of justice: reimagining political space in a globalizing world*, Columbia University Press, New York.

Gay, G 2000, *Culturally responsive teaching: Theory, research, and practice*, Teacher's College Press, New York.

Gillborn, D 2000, 'Anti-racism: From policy to praxis', In *Routledge International companion to education*, ed B Moon, S Brown & M Ben-Peretz, RoutledgeFalmer, London, pp. 476–488.

Hallinan, C & Judd, B 2012, 'Indigenous studies and race relations in Australian Sports', *Sport in Society*, Vol. 15, no. 7, pp. 915–921.

Hayes, D, Mills, M, Christie, P, & Lingard, B 2006 *Teachers and schooling making a difference: Productive pedagogies, assessment and performance*, Allen & Unwin, Crows Nest.Hickey, C 2008, 'Physical education, sport and hyper-masculinity in schools', *Sport, Education and Society*, Vol. 13, no. 2, pp. 147–161.

Hingangaroa Smith, G 2003, *Indigenous struggle for the transformation of education and schooling*, keynote address to the Alaskan Federation of Natives Convention, Anchorage, Alaska, October, 2003.

hooks, b 1994, *Teaching to transgress: Education as the practice of freedom*, Routledge, London.

Horton, P 2014, 'Pacific Islanders in professional rugby football: Bodies, minds and cultural continuities', *Asia Pacific Journal of Sport and Social Science*, Vol. 3, no. 3, pp. 222–235.

Kanu, Y 2007, 'Increasing school success among Aboriginal students: Culturally responsive curriculum or macrostructural variables affecting schooling?', *Diaspora, Indigenous, and Minority Education*, Vol.1, no. 1, pp. 21–41.

Kearney, A 2012, 'Indigeneity and the performance of corporeal masculinities in the Australian Football League', *Sport in Society*, Vol. 15, no. 7, pp. 936–951.

Keddie, A 2012, *Educating for diversity and social justice.* Routledge, New York.

Keddie, A. & Niesche, R. 2012, '"It's almost like a White school now": racialised complexities, Indigenous representation and school leadership', *Critical Studies in Education*, Vol. 53, no. 2, pp. 169–182.

Klenowski, V 2009, *Respecting local, cultural contexts for assessment practice in an era of globalization*, Springer Publishing Company, New York.

Ladson-Billings, G & Gillborn, D (eds) 2004, *The RoutledgeFalmer reader in multicultural education*, RoutledgeFalmer, London.

Lewthwaite, B & McMillan, B 2010, '"She can bother me, and that's because she cares": What Inuit students say about teaching and their learning', *Canadian Journal of Education*, Vol. 33, no. 1, pp. 140–175.

Luke, A 2009, 'On indigenous education', *Teaching Education*, Vol. 20, no. 1, pp. 1–5.

McConaghy, C 2000, *Rethinking indigenous education: Culturalism, colonialism, and the politics of knowing*, Post Pressed, Flaxton.

Messner, M 1992, *Power at play: Sports and the problem of masculinity*, Beacon Press, Boston, MA.

Mills, M 2001, *Challenging violence in schools: An issue of masculinities*, Open University Press, Buckingham.

Ministerial Council on Education, Employment, Training and Youth Affairs (MCEETYA). 2008, *Melbourne declaration on educational goals for young Australians*, State Government of Victoria. Available from: https://www.currculum.edu.au. [22 December 2014].

Mohanty, C 2003, *Feminism without borders.* Duke University Press, London.

Moreton-Robinson, A 1998, 'When the object speaks, a postcolonial encounter: Anthropological representations and Aboriginal women's self-presentations', *Discourse: Studies in the Cultural Politics of Education*, Vol. 19, no. 3, pp. 275–289.

Moreton-Robinson, A 2000, *Talkin' up to the white woman: Indigenous women and feminism.* University of Queensland Press, St Lucia.

Nakata, M 2007, 'The cultural interface', *The Australian Journal of Indigenous Education*, Vol. 36, pp. 7–14.

Nieto, S 1999, *The light in their eyes: Creating multicultural learning communities.* Teacher's College Press, New York.

Pearson, N 2009, *Radical Hope: education and equality in Australia*, Black Inc, Melbourne.

Queensland Government, Indigenous Education. Available online at http://indigenous.education.qld.gov.au/eatsips/Pages/default.aspx.

Reid, J & Santoro, N 2006, 'Cinders in Snow?: Indigenous teacher identities in formation', *Asia-Pacific Journal of Teachers Education*, Vol. 34, no. 2, pp. 143–160.

Ritchie, J 2008, 'Honouring Māori subjectivities within early childhood education in Aotearoa', *Contemporary Issues in Early Childhood*, Vol. 9, no. 3, pp. 202–210.

Santoro, N & Reid, J 2006, 'All things to all people': Indigenous teachers in the Australian teaching profession', *European Journal of Teacher Education*, Vol. 29, no. 3, pp. 287–303.

Sarra, C 2003, 'Cherbourg State School: Strong and smart', *What Works Program: Improving outcomes for Indigenous students.* Available from: http://www.whatworks.edu.au. [1 July 2012].

Sleeter, C 2005, *Un-standardizing curriculum.* Teachers' College Press, New York.

Spivak, G 1990, *The post-colonial critic: Interviews, strategies, dialogues*, Routledge, New York.

Spring, J 2003, *Deculturalization and the struggle for equality: A brief history of the education of dominated cultures in the United States*, McGraw Hill, New York.

Tamir, Yael 1999, 'Siding with the underdogs', In *Is multiculturalism bad for women?*, ed SM Okin & J Cohen, Princeton University Press, Princeton, NJ, pp. 7–20.

7 A politics of differentiation towards social justice

As researchers, we have spent many hours in schools and classrooms especially in Australia, but also across the UK and other parts of Europe. There are distinctive characteristics of the 'western' mainstream school and classroom that would be familiar to most and consistent across contexts, such as the organisation of reception areas, classrooms and staffrooms; the management of teachers through timetabling and students through disciplinary systems; and the delivery of pedagogy, curriculum and assessment. These familiar ways of doing school were evident at both Red Point High and Crimson High. At both schools there were distinct physical or spatial similarities, for example, at Red Point High like at Crimson High, the reception areas were achievement-oriented and celebratory. Walls were adorned with honours boards and photos celebrating the schools' accomplishments and cabinets were full of trophies and ribbons marking various sporting and academic awards. At both schools there were organisational and management similarities in terms of how teaching was grouped and timetabled according to subject area and how students were sanctioned for misbehaviour, whether through warnings, 'blue slips' or periods of time-out. At both schools there was a similar mixture of pedagogical approaches of varying quality and scope, with some teaching we considered to be outstanding in terms of engagement and intellectual rigour and other teaching less so.

At both schools we met a diversity of students; some were earnest and cheerful while others were bored and disengaged. Some clearly loved school, while others clearly didn't. At both schools we encountered hard working and dedicated educators and leaders doing their utmost to support the students within their schools. Many seemed passionate and determined while others appeared stressed and overworked. Many clearly loved their job, a few clearly didn't. All of these educators were grappling with the complex and difficult job that is education and schooling in contemporary times. All of them were engaging in a politics of differentiation shaped variously by their particular school contexts with varied implications for social justice. It is to these issues that this chapter turns.

In Chapter 1 of this book we described each of the schools drawing on Braun et al.'s (2010) heuristic device for thinking about the many facets of context that affect the way that schools interact with policy. Braun et al. (2010) argue that 'situated' (e.g. student intake and school history), 'professional' (e.g. teacher values and school ethos), 'material' (e.g. staffing and school budget) and 'external' (e.g. the pressures and expectations of tests and department policy) factors significantly impact on a school's capacities to cope with and respond to policy. As we argued in the first chapter, these factors matter in thinking about differentiation whether at the more structural level of the school or the more student-focused level of the classroom. Well-resourced schools with class privileged students and a history of high academic achievement will, for example, approach issues of differentiation in different ways from a school in a disadvantaged area that is less well-resourced. Approaches to differentiation will vary considerably within the ordinary or 'mainstream' school, such as those in Braun et al.'s (2010) research but also within the 'non-traditional' or alternative school (see Mills & McGregor 2014). These different approaches, influenced as they are by different contextual factors, will impact on a school's social justice priorities, practices and outcomes. A school with a culturally homogenous, high performing and privileged cohort will likely have different equity priorities than a school catering to an entirely Indigenous student cohort. In the former school, sustaining academic excellence through a focus on improving the outcomes of less academically able students might be an equity priority, while at the latter school cultural and political justice might be greater priorities. While variously taken up *within* these schools, the contextual disparities *between* these schools would likely generate a different politics of redistribution, recognition and representation that would also likely generate different tensions and problematics. Context provides a framework for understanding local practices and differences between schools, but we do not regard contextual factors as determining practices. Indeed, the chapters in this volume provide compelling examples of forms of agency exercised by teachers and principals to work around contextual constraints, to challenge established expectations within the school and to create new relationships with students and their communities. Our deployment of Braun's contextual heuristic, therefore, should be regarded as a device to describe and critique current practices in relation to possibilities for social justice. How these possibilities are taken up within schools requires equal attention to the agency of actors.

This book has highlighted tensions and problematics in how a politics of differentiation was engaged with at Red Point High and Crimson High. Both schools were concerned with and attempted to pursue social justice goals, and this was clear in their pedagogical and curricular approaches, their expectations and care towards learners and their extracurricular practices. Amid these approaches circulated a politics of recognition concerned with economic, cultural and political justice. Redistributive (economic justice) concerns, for example, could be seen in each school's focus on high expectations for academic achievement (so that all students can achieve the credentialing required to accrue the economic benefits of the social world) while recognitive (cultural justice) and representative (political justice) concerns could be seen in each of the school's focus on valuing Indigenous culture and voices. In each school, however, matters of context–in relation to situated, professional, material and external factors–were significant in how a politics of differentiation for social justice played out. This chapter is organised around these contextual factors, mindful of how they impact on social justice at each of the schools. Such organisation seeks to both draw together the key findings of the book and provide further insight into how schools might frame differentiation within their contexts to better align with social justice goals.

In this chapter we also draw out the threads associated with leadership that run through our accounts of each school. Phil's and Geoff's voices feature prominently throughout the book, and this is no accident. As leaders of Red Point High and Crimson High, we recognise how they powerfully shape the politics of differentiation in their schools in relation to social justice and the significance of their leadership in pursuing a socially just approach to student differentiation. However, at the same time, we recognise the ways in which both of these leaders were constrained and enabled by the particular discourses operating within their respective schools and by their length of time at the schools, by the experiences they brought to the school and by the ways in which their leadership practices were read by the broader school community.

Our drawing on the framings of Braun et al. (2010) in relation to context and Fraser (2008a; 2008b) in relation to social justice to present the book's key findings is not designed to reflect a structuralist or normative analysis. We do not see these ways of conceptualising context or justice in fixed or absolute ways. We recognise, for example, that schools, while bound by particular contextual factors, are also enabled by them and that these factors are dynamic in terms of historicity and sociality. These factors, as they are shaped by the social, are never immutable. What we try to do in this chapter is draw attention to the spaces of agency and constraint they offer in relation to social justice. Along these lines we understand Fraser's dimensions of social justice in our account as interpretive and reflective of the particular focus in this book on the politics of differentiation at Red Point High and Crimson High. We do offer an analysis of the ways in which each school intersects with matters of context in relation to Fraser's three dimensions of social justice towards the ideal of participatory parity for all. However, we do not understand these dimensions as polarised or separate from each other. They are, as Fraser (2008a; 2008b) argues, inter-imbricated and overlapping. Thus, while we draw on the frameworks of Braun et al. and Fraser as organising principles within which to draw together the book's key findings and themes, we also use them to proliferate new lines of thought and enquiry. Thus the final section of the book culminates in a set of key provocations based on the book's primary insights.

Red Point High

As we noted in Chapter 1, there were particular *situated* factors (intake and history) at Red Point High that impacted on the school's approach to differentiation. As a traditional school, it prided itself on academic excellence and high expectations in relation to behaviour, attendance and academic effort. This was certainly made possible by the demographic of the school's cohort, which mainly consisted of class and race-privileged students, and through its long history of catering to such students since its inception in the 1950s as one of the largest state high schools in the region. It can be said then that Red Point High's situated factors privileged this school–i.e. these factors placed it well to maintain its reputation as academically excellent and to continue to attract the 'best' students in the region. However, they also circumscribed what was possible for the new principal, Phil, to achieve when he sought to prioritise a social justice agenda related to Indigenous participation and recognition.

As we noted in Chapter 3, in our exploration of the politics around the school's high expectations, there were key tensions at Red Point High that impacted on social justice. In particular, the school's admissions protocol–its managed enrolment plan to restrict student numbers and its excellence programs–engaged in an exclusionary politics. For Phil, there were racialised dimensions to this politics in the resentment and concern some staff expressed in response to his attempts to increase the school's Indigenous student intake and promote a greater valuing of Indigenous culture. To be sure Phil explicitly challenged these exclusionary views but he was, in effect, attempting to challenge a long and perhaps taken-for-granted history of exclusionary differentiation in relation to intake. In terms of social justice, such differentiation can be interpreted as reproducing an inequitable status quo that privileges Whiteness and middle-classness. Such privileging reflects a sense of misrecognition and misrepresentation at Red Point High of marginalised groups (e.g. Indigenous groups in relation to a devaluing of their culture and a delegitimising of their voices). Following this, we can see how redistributive justice is also curtailed because access and participation at this school is delimited to a selective group who will benefit from its history of academic excellence and the privileged credentialing to which it will invariably lead (Fraser 2008a & 2008b; Mills & Gale 2010; Keddie 2012).

There were specific *professional* factors (associated with teacher values and matters of school ethos) at Red Point High that impacted on the school's approach to differentiation. As we outlined in Chapter 1 these factors were associated with the school's image or reputation of academic excellence. Creating and sustaining this image involved a particular set of values relating to strict codes of behaviour and school rules resonant of a private school (for example, the enforcing of uniform dress and strong disciplinary structures). Indeed, the teachers and broader staff at Red Point High were particularly proud of their reputation as aligning with these private school codes and rules. Alongside these values and also relating to the school's ethos were concerns with offering a broad and comprehensive curriculum and creating a caring and safe environment.

In Chapters 2, 3 and 4, we explored the complex and contested terrain surrounding these professional factors as they related to practices of differentiation. Such complexities were particularly apparent in: 1) the uncertainties expressed by teachers about how to define and approach differentiation in relation to pedagogy, 2) matters of academic achievement and ability streaming, and 3) matters of care in its institutionalised and affective forms. In Chapter 2 we highlighted teachers' confusion about what constitutes differentiation manifest in the various ways differentiation was understood and deployed to support students. The teachers critically reflected on their practices, such as creating individualised learning plans, peer coaching and grouping students in terms of ability or friendship. The overwhelming focus here was on organising the classroom and students towards improving academic outcomes. While variously successful, the forms of pedagogical differentiation foregrounded in this chapter reflected redistributive justice principles. An enabling politics of differentiation towards such principles was evident in teachers' efforts to ensure that all students, especially the 'low achievers', were challenged and supported to achieve academically.

In Chapter 3, however, we noted a disabling politics of differentiation in the ways that ability streaming at Red Point High was deployed. Streaming seemed to lead to a degraded pedagogy within lower-streamed classes that tended to cater for disadvantaged students and that tended to keep students quiet rather than extend them academically. The sorts of injustices that arise from ability streaming are well recognised (see Terwel 2005). They are particularly impactful in relation to curtailing redistributive justice in their likely reproduction of racialised and classed pathways of academic and future life success.

This disabling politics around streaming and deficit understandings was framed by and perhaps collided with the school's efforts to maintain its private school image of academic and behavioural excellence. Certainly, as we detailed in Chapter 4, care for the students tended to focus on performative goals and institutional care. To this extent, there were strong efforts to raise the performance of low achieving students that related to distant institutional care that was low in emotional investment and seemed more about maintaining the school's reputation of academic and behavioural excellence rather than caring for the individual student. As we suggested in Chapter 4, such forms of institutional care, when coupled with appropriate learner support, can reflect redistributive justice in terms of assisting marginalised students to achieve on the same measuring sticks of success as their more privileged counterparts (Fraser 2008a). They are, however, at odds with the academic immobility and low expectations that can arise from ability streaming which provides an interesting paradox at Red Point High (i.e. how does ability streaming reconcile with the school's emphasis on performative goals and institutional care?).

Such forms of institutional care are also at odds with the personal stories of care we detailed in Chapter 4, like the heart-wrenching account of a girl whose brother took his own life and who was supported by the Indigenous liaison officer to keep her promise to her brother that she would do better after his death by achieving a whole term without receiving a disciplinary 'blue slip'. Such stories, as we argued in this chapter, reflect the embodied and lived experience of teaching in schools that demand teachers' deep interest in their students' lives and especially a recognition of the complex factors that impact on students' capacities to be successful at school. In relation to care, there were also stories of solidarity at Red Point High–reflected in the principal's delight that three out of the five key student leadership positions at the school were occupied by Indigenous students. Such stories exemplify a politics of differentiation around caring and solidarity relations that move towards affective equality (Lynch 2010). However, as we also argued, this is a politics that is at odds with the broader privileging of institutionalised care at this school and very difficult to pursue amid current performative notions of what constitutes quality teachers and teaching that are far more consistent with institutionalised versions of care.

Material factors such as staffing and school budget had a significant impact on approaches to differentiation at Red Point High. Red Point High is a well-resourced school in relation to staffing, with 25 per cent of staff employed in a non-teaching capacity to support both teachers and students. The school employed a full-time Indigenous liaison officer, whose responsibility was to provide counselling, pastoral care, advocacy and learning support for the Indigenous students, and a school-based youth health nurse to support student and teacher wellbeing. These material factors are significant in their capacity to lead to improved social justice outcomes. Certainly, the employment of an education counsellor for the Indigenous students reflects the principles of political and cultural justice. There is the potential here to support greater parity of participation for these students through this appointment as it: 1) accords a voice to these marginalised groups in its focus on advocacy and pastoral care and 2) leads to opportunities of recognitive justice through a greater valuing of Indigenous culture. There were problematics associated with this representation; for example, the Indigenous liaison officer did not always feel that her voice was heard and she felt marginalised in relation to the rest of the staffing body. There are also dangers in such a role–that any problems with Indigenous kids are seen as her responsibility–rather than a shared and accountable responsibility of all staff.

These problematics point to the dangers that can arise with such appointments in relation to cultural reductionism and essentialism–dangers we explored in later chapters in relation to Crimson High. As we indicated in Chapter 6, and applicable here, we would actively and strongly support greater Indigenous representation and recognition in all aspects of schooling–whether through staffing, celebrating important events or other areas such as curriculum, pedagogy or assessment. These are key aspects of socially just schooling and, indeed, reflect the equity priorities that many Indigenous peoples seek–self-determination and cultural recognition (see The Coolangatta Statement 1999). We also note, as we explore further later in this chapter, the ways in which such representation and recognition can reproduce constructions of (Indigenous) difference as other and marginal and thus work to further cement inequities. Notwithstanding such contentions, the deployment of material resources at the school to support Indigenous students can certainly be seen as reflecting the principles of social justice. This deployment is particularly critical for a school such as Red Point High, given its locale within a community with a long and troubled history of racism and racialised politics.

Also enabling social justice was the school's strong focus on professional development in the area of differentiation. As we detailed in Chapter 2, the school provided material support so that teachers could participate in external seminars (around the work of Carol Tomlinson 1999; 2000; 2008) and internal workshops (as part of our study). As evident in this chapter, the teachers drew on the learnings from these seminars to critically reflect on and improve their practices of differentiation with matters of social justice (especially redistributive justice in supporting all learners to achieve academically) central to their concerns. Such critical reflection within the collaborative and reflective contexts of professional development would seem particularly important in generating a more socially just approach to differentiation at Red Point High–this is especially so given the lack of clarity and feelings of uncertainty around differentiation expressed by the teachers at this school.

The politics of differentiation deployed within Red Point High to support students was strongly shaped by specific *external* factors–i.e. the pressures of tests and departmental policy. As we noted in Chapter 1, the school embraced external measures of school effectiveness, and this was evident in their investments in raising their differentiation score on the Queensland Audit of Teaching and Learning. As a school of academic excellence with a private school image to uphold, external and public markers of success are particularly important whether they be in relation to attainment on a pedagogical audit or the school's performance on standardised tests and exams. While reductive and imposed, they are public representations that portend to capture a school's quality and effectiveness (see Ball 2003; Apple 2005). Thus, all schools are expected, like Red Point High, to invest in and provide evidence in relation to success on such markers if they are to be seen as doing the right things efficiently and in the correct way (Apple 2005). These are mechanisms of the audit culture that have wielded unmistakable political power in determining the legitimacy or otherwise of schools (Rose 1999). They encompass modes of regulation and surveillance that for some engender uncertainty and anxiety but for others the opportunity to forge a triumphant identity (see Ball 2003).

The embracing of these external measures of success at Red Point High seemed, for the most part, to reflect the latter. Perhaps this was because the school did very well on such markers and as such they offered an opportunity for it to mark itself out as outstanding and better than the rest (see Ball 2003; 2009; Keddie 2013). It can be said then that such external factors–i.e. the expectations and priorities of the audit culture–aligned nicely with the priorities at Red Point High. Thus the school did not need to shift its ethos and values to any great extent to fit with the priorities of the audit culture. It is fair to say that some of the school's practices of differentiation–e.g. in terms of its exclusionary politics to ensure it maintained its 'triumphant' status as academically and behaviourally excellent–could be seen as unhelpful or damaging. However, in the main, the school did not need to adopt further unhelpful or damaging practices to fit with broader audit priorities. Indeed, one outcome of the audit process was to challenge the staff to consider how they were value adding to students' learning rather than simply maintaining their entry levels of performance. And, of course, other contextual factors, such as its privileged demographics (situated) and resourcing (material), worked with these professional values to strengthen the school's capacity to hold its ground amid these priorities (Braun et al. 2010).

It is clear that Red Point High's relationship with these external pressures supports a redistributive approach to social justice (as earlier defined). However, as we noted in Chapter 2, for some teachers, external modes of regulation and surveillance did engender uncertainty and anxiety. This was most evident perhaps in the teachers' confusions and concerns about how they could better differentiate their practice so that all students could perform better on standardised tests, but also in some teachers' expressed concerns about the narrowness and prescription of current external measures of school success as inadequate in capturing its quality and worth. For some teachers at Red Point High, the priorities of the audit culture were seen as inhibiting their freedom to differentiate in relation to pedagogy and curriculum. They were, indeed, as well recognised in the broader literature, seen as degrading their pedagogy to a teach-to-the-test mentality and delimiting the quality and scope of curriculum. Thus, as we indicated in Chapter 2, there were clear tensions at Red Point High between embracing the external demands of the audit culture and providing meaningful pedagogical and curricular differentiation to support all students.

Crimson High

The *situated* factors at Crimson High that impacted on its approach to differentiation varied in many ways from those at Red Point High. Crimson High also prioritised high expectations in terms of academic and behavioural performance, but it took pride in its long history of being an inclusive school serving some of the most marginalised young people in the surrounding communities. This history was supported through a very long-term principal, Geoff, who was highly committed to the school and the principles of inclusivity. The identity 'school for all' was particularly appealing to him in capturing the school's inclusive tradition. Such inclusivity at Crimson High seemed to be demanded by the school's socially and culturally diverse demographic. Over 40 cultural groups are represented within this demographic, including a large Indigenous population. Evidence that the school was socially inclusive was perhaps most apparent in the recent rise in school attendance figures (especially within its Indigenous student cohort) and in high levels of parent satisfaction.

As we noted in Chapters 5 and 6 (and as we will detail further below), there were many tensions this school experienced in relation to its attempts to be a school for all, some enabling and some constraining in terms of social justice. Notwithstanding, it can be said that the politics of differentiation encompassed by the inclusive ethos at Crimson High supported the principles of economic, cultural and political justice. These principles were clearly evident in the responsibility the school accepted in educating the young Indigenous people from a nearby Island community after their high school program was closed down. As we noted in Chapter 1, this island originally served as a reserve to isolate Indigenous people who were deemed 'disruptive' or unlawful and, as we mentioned in Chapter 6, this community experienced very high levels of economic and social deprivation. Accepting and supporting students from this community reflects a differentiated politics towards social justice in terms of its potential to disrupt the broader racialised and classed status quo, where schools that are over-represented in terms of Indigeneity are seen negatively as 'Blackfella schools' (see Chapter 6).

For Geoff, being a school for Indigenous students was not a negative representation. The school's history and tradition of including the most marginalised students supports the principle of participatory parity, especially in relation to redistributive justice–i.e. these students are provided with the opportunity to access and accrue the benefits of a quality education just as their more privileged counterparts are. Such access and participation, as we detail in the next sections were, of course, crucial to pursuing other forms of justice (cultural and political) at this school. For, as we well know, without the inclusion and presence of the 'other', the other is often forgotten within dominant and taken-for-granted frames of privilege.

The *professional* factors of teacher values and school ethos at Crimson High greatly impacted on its approach to differentiation. Its focus on social inclusivity, as we noted in Chapter 1, was no doubt fostered by the strong vision of the long established leadership team whose employment at the school spanned many decades. In response to the diversity of its demographics, there was an enormous range of programs both curricular and extracurricular. Like Red Point High, Crimson High offered a broad and comprehensive curriculum and there were strong mechanisms in place to create a caring and safe environment. In particular, as we noted in Chapters 5 and 6, there was a focus on engaging students through music and sporting excellence programs that were especially targeted at disadvantaged groups who also tended to be low achievers. As we explored in Chapters 5 and 6, these programs (as with other initiatives at the school) were not only designed to engage students but they were also focused on broadening social and cultural awareness.

There were, of course, many tensions and complexities surrounding these professional factors and, in particular Crimson High's efforts to be a school for all. In Chapters 5 and 6, we foregrounded tensions and complexities associated with: 1) addressing low levels of academic and social engagement through differentiated curriculum; and 2) addressing cultural recognition through differentiating extracurricular programs. In Chapter 5 our focus was on curriculum differentiation. We highlighted the possibilities within a differentiated curriculum to engage and motivate students. We identified effective 'hooks', such as the music program, that we saw as potentially drawing disengaged students into the school and opening up possibilities for them to re-engage with the formal academic curriculum. We also noted, however, that such hooks, which can be devoid of 'powerful knowledges', may not lead to re-engagement and may, indeed, become corridors to 'nowhere'. Thus we noted that in some instances, attempts to become 'a school for all' can work in much the same way as streaming by not challenging students intellectually, or providing them with access to knowledges that have significant currency in the world of further education. In this respect, such curriculum differentiation may work against the most marginalised students. However, we also explored how a broad curriculum like the one at Crimson High could reflect redistributive justice as a hook to potentially re-engage students in the broader academic curriculum and enhance their access to powerful knowledge. Furthermore, as we argued in this chapter, this curriculum also reflected representative (political) justice as an avenue where these disengaged students were accorded a voice and a sense of self-determination in their school lives.

Chapter 6 was similarly focused on engaging learners, but the emphasis here was on issues of cultural recognition and the differentiation of extracurricular activities. We highlighted the significance of educators being critically aware of how they construct race and use it as an organising principle in their work. In relation to Crimson High such awareness was apparent in the sensitivity of staff to the broader racialised politics impacting on the school, like the negative 'Blackfella' tag, and in their efforts to overcome racism through particular programs focused on recognising and valuing Indigenous culture and voices. We argued in this chapter that such Indigenous-focused initiatives are significant in their potential to lead to cultural and political justice for Indigenous people. Indeed, they are central to pursuing the Indigenous equity priorities of self-determination and cultural recognition. What we tried to highlight in this chapter is that such initiatives are not unproblematic and can be vulnerable to cultural essentialising, where Indigeneity is positioned as 'other' in ways that wash out the complexity and multiplicity of Indigenous identities and that delimit who can speak for and about Indigenous issues. These ways of constructing Indigeneity can work to set up a false binary where Indigeneity is positioned as incommensurable with Whiteness. Consistent with much of the critical multiculturalism literature, we were concerned here with how such initiatives may unwittingly play into rather than transform broader racialised inequities.

In Chapter 6 we also highlighted the importance of recognising the multiplicity and complexity of culture and rejecting binary understandings of race that privilege Whiteness. We highlighted the potential of the sports program (and in particular football) to support a broadening of students' cultural and social awareness and understandings of difference to ameliorate (in this case) hostilities between Indigenous and Maori boys. In this context, the rich complexities and contradictions of Indigenous (and other marginalised) identities were acknowledged in ways that did not presume fixed or static notions of culture. In this respect, this chapter drew attention to the possibilities but also problematics associated with cultural recognition and more specifically the reality that there are times when it is appropriate to draw on notions of 'Indigenous culture' to enable possibilities for Indigenous people but that such notions can be limiting and exclusionary and that there are other forms of recognition, such as the football activity, that might be equally positive and socially just.

Like at Red Point High, the *material* factors at Crimson High were highly productive in supporting a socially just approach to differentiation. The school was similarly well resourced in terms of non-teaching/ancillary staff, with a wellbeing team and a range of proactive programs that supported the various academic, social and physical needs of students. The social justice implications of such support were many–for example, the 'engagement team' created to build relationships between the school and students from disadvantaged backgrounds through home visits supported redistributive principles of justice through ensuring access and participation for these students to a quality education. There was also strong support at Crimson High, as with Red Point High, for teacher professional development on a range of different schooling issues including differentiation. There was a particular focus here on supporting beginning teachers. In relation to reflecting the principles of recognitive and representative justice, all new staff were required to undertake cultural awareness training with a particular focus on Indigeneity led by and involving the Indigenous Support Staff.

As at Red Point High, the politics of differentiation at Crimson High were strongly informed by the *external* factors of the audit culture. Crimson High was enthusiastic in its engagement with external indicators of success and in improving its rating on these indicators. They provided evidence and public recognition of the school's achievements, which were many, varied and impressive. As we noted in Chapter 1, the school had won numerous major cultural and academic awards. It was also accredited by a number of other bodies such as Microsoft. The school's embracing of these external factors could be seen as providing an opportunity to mark itself out as outstanding (Ball 2003). Crafting this successful identity in relation to these external markers seemed at this school to be particularly significant given the high levels of disadvantage experienced by many of its students. It was central to stimulating these students' aspirations about what is possible in terms of their future lives and broadening opportunities for them in this respect. While perhaps the school's ethos deviated a little from the narrow priorities of the audit culture (in its strong focus on cultural/social learning), such deviation was not a concern at Crimson High. Despite the school performing slightly less well than some other schools on external measures of quality and effectiveness such as standardised tests, it maintained its inclusive and socially focused ethos. Indeed, this ethos, rather than being seen to detract from achievement on these measures, was seen as crucial to enabling them (as Geoff suggested in Chapter 6, without this school's inclusive ethos and 'hooks' like those within the sports and music programs, some of the more disengaged and disadvantaged students wouldn't come to school). This reflects, as we noted in Chapter 1, the school's critical approach to reform in terms of discerning and shaping their responses to policy to suit the ethos of the school and the needs of its students. The meaningful curricular and pedagogical differentiation within the sporting and music programs at Crimson High seems to exemplify this discerning.

Leadership, social justice and the politics of differentiation

In this section we draw together what we view as some of the distinctive threads within this book around issues of leadership with a specific focus on what we see as the key future challenges associated with school leadership and social justice amid current school reform priorities. As principals of Red Point High and Crimson High, Phil and Geoff powerfully shape the politics of differentiation in their schools in relation to social justice. As we have detailed in this chapter in relation to specific situated, professional, material and external factors, their leadership strongly impacts on how differentiation is approached with specific implications for social justice. As we noted earlier, both schools' pursuit of social justice is clear in their differentiation of pedagogy, curricular and extracurricular activities to support marginalised and disadvantaged students and in their differentiated approach to caring for these students. Phil's and Geoff's leadership is significant in shaping this differentiation to foster economic, cultural and political justice. Both these leaders set the stage for redistributive justice in their efforts to ensure that all students achieve academically regardless of their backgrounds, and both are champions of recognitive and representative justice in their focus on valuing Indigenous culture and voices. While, in each school, there were matters of context that impacted on Phil's and Geoff's vision for social justice, this vision is nonetheless consistent across both contexts and in many ways equally strong.

Maintaining this focus on socially just leadership in the current reform environment presents particular challenges and problematics. As we have already articulated in relation to each school's interaction with external factors, the priorities and pressures of the audit culture work in many ways to compromise social justice goals. They narrow school priorities and reduce school success to that which can be measured (e.g. standardised tests), they promote competition between schools, they degrade pedagogy to a teach-to-the-test mentality, they stifle curricular creativity and they place enormous pressure on teachers to focus solely on performative goals. It can also be said, however, that these priorities can lead to positive outcomes, for example, in enabling schools to more accurately identify and provide resources to particular groups of students who are underachieving so that they can perform better on the measures that count. Such priorities can thus work in socially just ways; however, as much research in schools has highlighted, they tend to align with a very narrow view about the purpose of schools and schooling (see Apple 2005; Ball 2003; Cranston et al. 2010). In particular they are focused on private rather than public goals. Where private goals are associated with employment credentialing and social mobility, public goals are associated with the public good and developing active and informed citizens. A focus on both private and public goals has long been a central mandate of contemporary schooling (see MCEETYA 2008). However, the priorities of the audit culture as they are aligned with private goals have sidelined the public purposes of schooling. For the educators in this book, including Phil and Geoff, this sidelining is resisted in their attempts to maintain a focus in their schools on social learning within broader parameters that do not value this emphasis.

Amid increasingly narrow external measures about what constitutes quality schooling, there is another key external factor that school leaders across the globe are grappling with, and that is the responsibilities of managing their schools within increasingly autonomised education systems. Policy and practice relating to school autonomy across western contexts is far from new of course. In Australia, for example, school autonomy was promoted over 40 years ago in the Karmel Report, and self-managing-schools have been part of the education landscape in the state of Victoria since the early 1990s. There has, however, been renewed emphasis on this reform agenda and the belief that granting schools greater freedom in governance and decision-making will promote community responsiveness, innovation and resource efficiency which will, in turn, improve the public education system overall (Cobbold 2014; Gobby 2013). Commitment to this idea is evident at a global policy level, where influential organisations such as the OECD (2011) have endorsed school autonomy as key to improving student performance.

Relevant to school leadership in the contexts where our study was carried out is the most recent iteration of school autonomy policy in Australia, the Independent Public Schools (IPS) initiative introduced in Queensland in 2013 (adopted from the Western Australian model that was introduced there in 2010). Indeed, since finishing our data collection, both Red Point High and Crimson High have converted from being 'regular' State High Schools to being IP schools. Thus they now have greater control and flexibility in relation to governance, matters of staffing, curriculum offerings and educational innovation than they otherwise had. They also enjoy increased direct resourcing from the state government and greater discretion in terms of how they use their funds (The State of Queensland 2014). For leaders of IP schools like Phil and Geoff, such freedoms would likely be very welcome and highly useful in supporting their schools to pursue their improvement efforts, including those associated with social justice. However, such 'freedoms' of course will be very much shaped and tempered by the demands of the audit culture and its increasingly high-stakes accountabilities.

For many commentators, these demands are at odds with encouraging an equitable or socially just take up of school autonomy because they fuel competition between schools and compel schools to focus excessively on narrow measures of academic accountability. Such conditions clearly undermine the notion of schooling as a public good (Ball 2003; Cranston et al. 2010) and many of the social justice principles that we have focused on in this book. Working against these demands and the narrow foci they compel will, we contend, require leaders like Phil and Geoff to maintain a 'morally' focused approach to leadership in how they take up the freedoms of school autonomy reform (see Fullan 2002; Keddie 2015; Smyth 2011). For Fullan (2002), such leadership is about much more than just improving students' achievements on narrow performance measures. It is about engaging with a broad view of the purposes of schooling in terms of pursuing equity and citizenship goals. In relation to equity, this will entail leaders in Phil's and Geoff's position using their greater autonomy to promote rather than undermine equity and social justice through, for example, using their flexibility in terms of additional resources and staffing to support disadvantaged students and using curricular flexibility to maintain a focus on social and citizenship learning (see Keddie 2015).

The point here is that autonomy in the current environment can be taken up in a myriad of different ways. It can both open up and close down opportunities for working in socially just ways. Set against the backdrop of the audit culture, a key future challenge for principals like Phil and Geoff will be how they can negotiate a morally focused leadership in this space where 'educational goals [are] defined and framed on their underlying importance, not by whether or not they can be easily measured' (Cranston et al. 2010, p.535). These understandings will be instrumental in schools combining autonomy and accountability in socially just ways towards creating an equitable education system for all (see Dingerson 2008).

In the spirit of further articulating the key challenges confronting educators who seek to differentiate their practice in ways that support social justice, we turn now to the final section of the book, a set of provocations based on the book's primary insights.

Provocations

Schools and education systems are located within contexts of uncertainty and rapid social change. Amid this uncertainty questions of equity and social justice continually change and thus should continually be re-thought through critical engagement. There is no neat script or how-to list for directing educators to deploy a politics of differentiation for social justice. While educators might pursue economic, cultural and political justice in their schools and classrooms, such pursuit will, as we have been at pains to highlight in this book, be extremely varied, contextually located and politically informed and, of course, highly fraught! As such, we recognise that there are no easy answers or prescriptions for engaging a socially just politics of differentiation. What is certain is that working in such ways will generate many difficult and interesting provocations that must be worked through in the ways that the educators in this book have done. We offer the following key provocations as questions. They are organised around Fraser's three dimensions of social justice and focus on some of the most prominent issues raised in this book–matters of school identity, pedagogy, care, curriculum and extracurricular activities and staffing.

A politics of redistributive justice

School identity differentiation

- How can schools work against a politics of enrolment exclusion in light of the external demands of the audit culture that promote competition between schools in relation to success on standardised academic tests?

Pedagogical differentiation

- How can schools work within the external demands of the audit culture to provide meaningful pedagogical and curricular differentiation that supports all students?
- How can ability streaming be negotiated to support academic mobility and high expectations?

Differentiation and care

- How can a politics of institutionalised care (that aligns with the demands of the audit culture) work alongside (rather than disable) a politics of affective care?

Curriculum differentiation

- How can we trouble the current hierarchical constructions of knowledge that privilege particular subjects and marginalise others?
- Is a 'school for all' compatible with the policy of differentiated educational provision?

A politics of representative justice

Curriculum differentiation

- How can curriculum be differentiated to engage students in ways that support a hook to 'somewhere' rather than a corridor to 'nowhere'? How can we connect with, but also broaden, students' interests so that they have access to the powerful knowledge necessary for them to accrue the benefits of the social world?

Staffing

- How do we represent marginalised groups through inclusive staffing practices without essentialising voices from these groups and without delimiting who can speak and know on behalf of marginalised groups?

Pedagogy

- How can we privilege student voice in schooling environments that tend to be hyper-rational and controlling? How can we accord all students (even those who do not wish to speak) a voice? How can we avoid homogenising the student voice in our efforts to be inclusive?

A politics of recognitive justice

Pedagogy

- How can teachers deploy pedagogies that recognise and value but do not essentialise difference? What differences matter? Are some differences more 'valuable' than others? Who should determine what differences matter?

Curriculum, pedagogy and other schooling processes

- When might it be appropriate to draw on notions of 'culture' to enable possibilities for marginalised groups, and when might such markers work to limit and exclude these possibilities?
- How can we talk about or recognise marginalised knowledges such as Indigenous knowledges without bounding them and positioning them as other? What are 'authentic' cultural knowledges?

These are only some of the many provocations around matters of differentiation and social justice that educators are confronted with on a daily basis in their schools and classrooms. Many educators, as we have illustrated in this book, are struggling with these provocations and reconciling them with varied effects in terms of social justice. Perhaps the most salient message we can offer from their struggles is to reiterate the significance of a self-conscious, critical and contingent approach to differentiating for social justice. Understanding difference in nuanced and complex ways is necessary for 'intervening productively' within and against unjust schooling processes–and such understandings, like these provocations, must work against a 'politics of certainty'. Spaces for social justice within classrooms, schools and broader education systems will be opened up by a politics that recognises context and seeks economic, cultural, political and affective justice and also by a politics that continually questions itself to proliferate new lines of thought and enquiry.

References

Apple, M 2005, 'Education, markets and an audit culture', *Critical Quarterly*, Vol. 47, nos. 1–2, pp. 11–29.

Ball, S 2003, 'The teacher's soul and the terrors of performativity', *Journal of Education Policy*, Vol. 18, no. 2, pp. 215–228.

Braun, A, Maguire, M, & Ball, S 2010, 'Policy enactments in the UK Secondary School: Examining policy, practice and school positioning', *Journal of Education Policy*, Vol. 25, no. 4, pp. 547–560.

Cobbold, T 2014, *Pyne's school autonomy myth, Save our Schools:* Available from: http://www.saveourschools.com.au. [11 May 2014].

The Coolangatta Statement on Indigenous People's Rights in Education. 1999. *Journal of American Indian Education*, Vol, 39, no. 1, pp. 52–64.

Cranston, N, Mulford B, Keating J, et al. 2010, 'Primary school principals and the purposes of schooling in Australia,' *Journal of Educational Administration*, Vol. 48, no. 4, pp. 517–539.

Dingerson, L 2008, 'Unlovely: How the market is failing the children of New Orleans', In *Keeping the promise? The debate over Charter School*, ed L Peterson & B Miner, Rethinking Schools, Milwaukee WI, pp. 17–35.

Dingerson, L Peterson, B & B Miner (eds) 2008, *Keeping the promise? The debate over charter schools*. Milwaukee: Rethinking Schools Ltd.

Fraser, N 2008a, 'Rethinking recognition: overcoming displacement and reification in cultural politics', In *Adding Insult to Injury: Nancy Fraser debates her critics*, ed K Olson, Verso, London, pp. 129–141.

Fraser, N 2008b, 'Reframing justice in a globalising world', In *Adding Insult to Injury: Nancy Fraser debates her critics*, ed K Olson, Verso, London, pp. 273–294.

Fullan, M 2002 'The change leader', *Educational Leadership*, Vol. 59, no. 8, pp. 16–21.

Gobby, B 2013, 'Enacting the Independent Public Schools program in Western Australia', *Issues in Educational Research*, Vol. 23, no. 1, pp. 19–34.

Keddie, A 2012, *Educating for diversity and social justice*, Routledge, New York.

Keddie, A 2013, 'Thriving amid the performative demands of the contemporary audit culture: A matter of school context', *Journal of Education Policy*, Vol. 28, no. 6, pp. 750–766.

Keddie, A 2015, 'School autonomy as "the way of the future": Issues of equity, public purpose and moral leadership', *Educational Management Administration and Leadership*, DOI: 10.1177/1741143214559231.

Lynch, K 2010, 'Affective equality: Love, care and solidarity as productive forces in *Proceedings from GEXcel. CFS Report Series; No. 14: Tema Genus Report Series; No. 12*, ed S Strid & AG Jónasdóttir. Available from: http://researchrepository.ucd.ie. [13 November 2013].

Mills, C & Gale, T 2010, *Schooling in disadvantaged communities*, Springer, New York.
Mills, M & McGregor, G 2014, *Re-engaging young people in education: Learning from alternative schools*, Routledge, London.
Ministerial Council on Education, Employment, Training and Youth Affairs (MCEETYA) 2008, 'Melbourne Declaration on educational goals for young Australians', Government of Victoria.
OECD 2011, 'School autonomy and accountability: Are they related to school performance?' *PISA in Focus 9*, Available from: http://www.oecd.org. [6 May 2014].
Rose, N 1999, *Powers of freedom: Reframing political thought*, Cambridge University Press, Cambridge.
Smyth, J 2011, 'The disaster of the "self-managing school"–Genesis, trajectory, undisclosed agenda and effects', *Journal of Educational Administration and History*, Vol. 43, no. 2, pp. 95–117.
The State of Queensland 2014, *Independent public schools*, State of Queensland, Available from: http://education.qld.gov.au. [4 May 2014].
Terwel, J 2005, 'Curriculum differentiation: Multiple perspectives and developments in education', *Journal of Curriculum Studies*, Vol. 37, no. 6, pp. 653–670.Tomlinson, CA 1999, 'Mapping a route toward differentiated instruction', *Educational Leadership*, Vol. 57, no. 1, pp. 12–16.
Tomlinson, CA 2000, 'Reconcilable differences', *Educational Leadership*, Vol. 58, no. 1, pp. 6–11.
Tomlinson, CA 2008, 'Goals of differentiation', *Educational Leadership*, Vol. 66, no. 3, pp. 26–30.

Index